# YOUR recipe could appear in our next cookbook!

Share your tried & true family favorites with us instantly at

## www.gooseberrypatch.com

If you'd rather jot 'em down by hand, just mail this form to...
Gooseberry Patch • Cookbooks – Call for Recipes
PO Box 812 • Columbus, OH 43216-0812

## If your recipe is selected for a book, you'll receive a FREE copy!

*Please share only your original recipes or those that you have made your own over the years.*

Recipe Name:

Number of Servings:

Any fond memories about this recipe? Special touches you like to add
or handy shortcuts?

Ingredients (include specific measurements):

Instructions (continue on back if needed):

Special Code: **cookbookspage**

*Over* ➤

*Extra space for recipe if needed:*

## Tell us about yourself...

Your complete contact information is needed so that we can send you your FREE cookbook, if your recipe is published. Phone numbers and email addresses are kept private and will only be used if we have questions about your recipe.

Name:
Address:
City:                               State:            Zip:
Email:
Daytime Phone:

Thank you! Vickie & Jo Ann

# FaRMhouse chRiStmas

## Gooseberry Patch

An imprint of Globe Pequot
246 Goose Lane
Guilford, CT 06437

# www.gooseberrypatch.com
# 1•800•854•6673

Copyright 2017, Gooseberry Patch 978-1-62093-242-1

Photo Edition is a major revision of *Farmhouse Christmas*.

## Do you have a tried & true recipe...

tip, craft or memory that you'd like to see featured in a **Gooseberry Patch** cookbook? Visit our website at **www.gooseberrypatch.com** and follow the easy steps to submit your favorite family recipe.
Or send them to us at:

Gooseberry Patch
PO Box 812
Columbus, OH 43216-0812

Don't forget to include the number of servings your recipe makes, plus your name, address, phone number and email address. If we select your recipe, your name will appear right along with it... and you'll receive a **FREE** copy of the book!

# Contents

Farmhouse Breakfasts . . . . . 5

Home~Style Beginnings . . . .29

Fireside Soups & Breads . . . 63

Cozy Kitchen Suppers . . . . .89

Homemade Desserts . . . . . 119

Holiday Trimmings . . . . . .149

Christmas Past . . . . . . . . .169

Holiday Magic for Kids . . .183

Homespun Handiworks . . .197

# Dedication

Thank you to our family & friends
who remind us that the finest
gifts & greatest joys come from
the heart.

# Appreciation

To everyone who enjoys
the sound of sleigh bells,
the crunch of snow underfoot
and a night sky lit by
a winter moon.

# Apple Puff Flapjacks

*Julie Dobson*
*Loma Linda, CA*

*This is perfect for Christmas morning or any special breakfast!*

6 eggs
1-1/2 c. milk
1 c. all-purpose flour
3 T. sugar
1 t. vanilla
1/2 t. salt

1/4 t. cinnamon
1 stick margarine, melted
3 Granny Smith apples, peeled
   and thinly sliced
2 to 3 T. brown sugar
powdered sugar

Preheat oven to 425 degrees. In blender, mix eggs, milk, flour, sugar, vanilla, salt and cinnamon until blended; set aside. Pour margarine into a 13"x9" pan and add apple slices evenly to the dish. Return to oven until margarine sizzles. Do not let apples brown. Pour batter over apples. Sprinkle with brown sugar. Bake on the middle oven rack at 425 for 20 minutes or until puffed and brown. Dust with powdered sugar to taste. Serve immediately. Makes 6 to 8 servings.

Make a beautiful fireplace swag by attaching pine cones to a garland of greenery then wire on bunches of mistletoe, juniper berries and holly. Suspend it from your mantel with stocking hangers.

# Hearty Farmhouse Breakfasts

## Blueberry French Toast

*Gloria Kaufmann*
*Orrville, OH*

*This is a very refreshing dish to serve for breakfast...one of our daughter's favorites! We enjoy having overnight guests and when they visit, this is a favorite I serve them.*

2 c. fresh or frozen blueberries
2 T. cornstarch
1/2 c. orange juice
1/4 c. sugar
1/2 c. plus 3 T. water, divided

3 eggs, beaten
6 slices bread
2 T. butter, melted
cinnamon sugar

Place blueberries in a 13"x9" baking pan. Blend cornstarch, orange juice, sugar and 1/2 cup of water together and place over blueberries. In shallow dish or pie pan, beat eggs and 3 tablespoons of water together. Dip slices of bread in egg mixture, allowing time for bread to absorb eggs, then place on top of blueberries. Brush bread with butter. Sprinkle with cinnamon sugar. Bake in 350 degree oven for 15 to 20 minutes or until bread is lightly toasted and blueberries are bubbly and thickened.

*Homemade shortbread cookies tied with colorful ribbon look beautiful hanging in your windowpanes.*

# Fieldstone Farm Popovers

*Vickie*

*Emily loves these warm from the oven with butter and jam!*

| 2 eggs | 1 c. all-purpose flour |
| 1 c. milk | 1/2 t. salt |

Heat oven to 400 degrees. Butter 8 custard cups and place in oven on a baking sheet while preparing batter. Beat eggs slightly and add remaining ingredients. Beat mixture on medium speed for one minute, scraping sides of bowls. Batter should be smooth and thin. Remove custard cups from oven and fill each custard cup 1/3 full. Bake for 50 minutes, or until crisp and golden-brown. Do not open oven during baking time, or popovers may fall.

Old-fashioned glass canning jars are perfect for holding gifts from your kitchen! Fill them with your favorite dry mixes like hazelnut cocoa or your favorite layered cookie mix. You can also give jars filled with hearty homemade soup or friendship bread starter.

## Christmas Morn Sausage Rolls

*Kathy Horine*
*Louisville, KY*

*I always prepare these on Christmas Eve then put them in the oven on Christmas morning!*

2 8-oz. tubes of crescent rolls
1 lb. sausage, cooked and
   crumbled

1/2 c. Cheddar cheese, shredded

Preheat oven to 375 degrees. Separate tubes of rolls into 8 rectangles. Press diagonal seams together with a fork. Sprinkle rolls with sausage and cheese. Roll dough jelly-roll style. Slice rolls in half and place on cookie sheet, seam side down. Bake 15 to 20 minutes. Makes 16 rolls.

Invite your neighbors over for a holiday breakfast. Welcome them with steaming mugs of cider, Christmas music and a crackling fire. Serve hearty favorites buffet-style and chat about your holiday plans. It's a fun way to enjoy each others company!

# Mom's Granola

*Julie Dobson*
*Loma Linda, CA*

*My husband believes that if there is no homemade granola in the house, there is nothing for breakfast!*

7 c. uncooked oats
1 c. wheat germ
1 c. shredded coconut
1/2 c. brown sugar
1/2 c. oil

1/2 c. water
1 T. vanilla extract
1 t. salt
1 c. slivered almonds
1/2 c. pecans

Mix all ingredients thoroughly and bake in a shallow pan at 275 degrees for approximately one hour, or until coconut is slightly browned. Cool. Store in refrigerator. Makes 18 to 20 servings.

Attach a vintage Christmas card to the front of a small brown paper bag. Tuck in an old-fashioned glass jar filled with homemade granola and tie bag closed with a homespun bow. Present your early morning gift in a pretty market basket.

## Wintertime Spice Tea

*Mary Beth Smith*
*St. Charles, MO*

*This is quite a favorite at our home. For Christmas gifts, I make several batches, place in decorated bags tied with raffia and tuck in the recipe. It's always a nice gift for teachers, friends and neighbors.*

| | |
|---|---|
| 1 c. sweetened lemonade mix | 1-3/4 c. sugar |
| 1/2 c. instant tea | 1/2 t. cinnamon |
| 1 c. powdered orange drink mix | 1/2 t. cloves |

Mix all dry ingredients together and store in an airtight container. To serve, add 3 to 4 teaspoons to one cup of hot water, stir well. If giving as a gift, be sure to include the recipe.

Fill a galvanized bucket with pebbles. Tuck in a variety of spring-blooming bulbs...tulips, daffodils or hyacinths are all pretty! Add water around the pebbles, just barely covering them, and tie on a raffia bow. In just a few weeks you'll have a springtime bouquet.

# Old-Fashioned Baked Eggs

*Jana Warnell*
*Kalispell, MT*

*I always make this recipe for special occasions and anytime I have
friends over for brunch, it's always a huge success!*

16 eggs, beaten
1 c. half-and-half
2 c. ham, diced
1 T. chives, chopped

3/4 c. sour cream
1-1/2 c. Cheddar cheese, grated
2 T. butter, melted
salt and pepper, to taste

Add all ingredients in a large bowl; mix well. Pour into a buttered
13"x9" pan. Bake at 350 degrees for 45 minutes or until mixture
is set and top is golden. When done, knife inserted in center should
come out clean.

Dress up the kids' table
with white butcher's
paper, add crayon "place
mats!" Leave the crayons
on the table, and while
they're waiting to eat,
the kids can add their
own holiday designs.

## Sausage Quiche

*Julie Miller*
*Columbus, OH*

*This tasty and rich quiche recipe was shared with me by my mom.*

9-inch pie crust, unbaked
1 T. butter, melted
1 lb. fresh, mild pork sausage,
  browned and drained
1 T. all-purpose flour

1/2 c. Monterey Jack cheese,
  grated
2 lg. or 3 sm. eggs, beaten
1-1/2 c. milk

Brush pie crust with butter and bake for 20 minutes in a 350 degree oven. Mix sausage with flour. Sprinkle cheese on bottom of pie crust. Add sausage on top of cheese. Blend eggs and milk together. Pour over meat and cheese mixture. Return to oven and bake 30 to 35 minutes more or until knife comes out clean.

*Dress your holiday table for winter...use whimsical mittens to hold your napkins and silverware and lay woolen scarves across the table to serve as placemats. Enamelware plates and cups add a rustic charm.*

# Cherry Coffeecake

*Gloria Kaufmann*
*Orrville, OH*

*This is a recipe I often serve. Although this can be made ahead, it is wonderful served warm.*

1 box yellow cake mix, divided
2 eggs
2/3 c. warm water
2 pkgs. instant dry yeast

1 c. all-purpose flour
21-oz. can cherry pie filling
5 T. margarine, melted

Mix 1-1/2 cups cake mix with eggs, water, yeast and flour. Beat for 2 minutes. Spread into 13"x9" pan. Top with pie filling. In a separate bowl, mix remaining cake mix with margarine until mixture is crumbly and sprinkle on top of pie filling. Bake at 375 degrees for 30 minutes.

## Glaze:

1 c. powdered sugar
1 T. water

1 T. corn syrup

Mix all ingredients together and drizzle over warm cake.

# Hearty Farmhouse Breakfasts

## Applesauce Pancakes

*Kristi Warzocha*
*Lakewood, OH*

*These are wonderful on a cold winter's morning!*

1 c. all-purpose flour, sifted
1 T. sugar
1-1/2 t. baking powder
1/2 t. salt
1/4 t. cinnamon
1 c. applesauce

1/4 t. orange zest, grated
1/4 t. vanilla extract
2 egg yolks, beaten
1 T. butter, melted
2 egg whites
Garnish: lemon zest strips

Sift together dry ingredients into a large mixing bowl. Blend in applesauce, orange zest, vanilla, egg yolks and butter. Beat egg whites until stiff but not dry, then fold into batter. Ladle batter onto a lightly oiled hot griddle, to desired pancake size. Cook until small bubbles form throughout, then turn to brown the other side. Garnish if desired.

## Apple Cider Syrup:

2 c. apple cider
1-1/2 c. brown sugar

1-inch cinnamon stick
1-1/2 t. whole cloves

Combine ingredients in a saucepan. Bring to a boil, lower heat to medium, and cook until liquid is reduced to about half, forming syrup. Remove spices; serve warm.

*Oh the snow, the beautiful snow! Filling the sky and the earth below!*

*—J. W. Watson*

# French Toast Waffles

*Jo Ann*

*If you need to reheat, just pop in the toaster!*

| | |
|---|---|
| 1/2 c. milk | 1/2 t. salt |
| 4 eggs | 2 T. butter, melted |
| 1 T. sugar | 8 to 10 slices of bread |

Preheat waffle iron. Spray with a light coating of vegetable oil. In a shallow bowl, combine milk, eggs, sugar and salt, then melted butter. Dip bread slices, one at a time, in egg mixture. Bake in waffle iron 2 to 3 minutes or until brown. Top with strawberry butter.

## Strawberry Butter:

1/2 lb. butter, softened
10-oz. pkg. frozen strawberries,
    thawed and drained
1/2 c. powdered sugar

Combine all ingredients in a mixer or food processor until smooth and creamy. Serve at room temperature.

*A muffin tin filled with votives, tea lights tucked into pudding molds and candles hidden inside an old-fashioned grater make a wonderful tabletop display. Add some gingerbread men, fragrant evergreen boughs and vintage kitchen utensils.*

## Dutch Babies

*Betsy Priester*
*Franklinville, NY*

*In the winter, my family tops these with warm apple pie filling.*

1 c. milk
1 c. all-purpose flour
4 eggs
1 t. vanilla

1 stick margarine, melted
powdered sugar, maple syrup or
    other honey

Combine milk, flour, eggs and vanilla. Place margarine in 13"x9" pan. Pour mixture into pan and bake at 400 degrees for 20 minutes or until golden brown and puffy. Serve with your favorite topping.

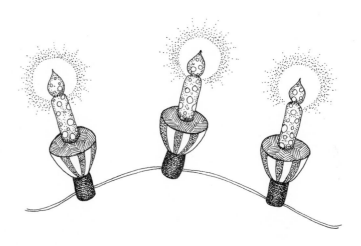

If you're planning a family get-together, decorate your table to bring back childhood memories. Use old-fashioned bubble lights and greenery as a table centerpiece and glue photocopies of old family photos to heavy paper for personalized place cards.

# Buttermilk-Raisin Buns

*Becky Sykes*
*Gooseberry Patch*

*Top these with your favorite fruit.*

3 to 3-1/2 c. all-purpose flour
1 T. baking powder
1/2 t. salt
2 t. margarine
1 c. nonfat buttermilk
3 egg whites

1-1/2 c. golden raisins
3/4 c. unsweetened applesauce
2 t. cinnamon
2 T. strawberry fruit spread,
   melted

Preheat oven to 400 degrees. Spray a 13"x9" baking pan with cooking spray. Combine flour, baking powder and salt in a large bowl. Cut in margarine with pastry blender until mixture resembles fine crumbs. Mix in buttermilk and egg whites. Turn dough onto lightly floured surface; gently knead in enough additional flour until dough is no longer sticky and is easy to handle. Roll dough into an 8-inch square. Mix raisins, applesauce and cinnamon; spread over dough. Roll dough jelly-roll style; pinch edge of dough into roll to seal. Cut into 8 slices and place slices one inch apart in pan. Bake 20 to 25 minutes or until lightly browned. Brush with fruit spread, remove from pan and let cool on wire rack. Makes 8 buns.

String an assortment of ribbon candy onto a holiday wreath. Your family will love to snip off a treat!

## Raspberry Muffins

*Pat Habiger*
*Spearville, KS*

*I love raspberries, and these muffins are especially tasty!*

3 c. all-purpose flour
1 c. sugar
4 t. baking powder
1 t. salt
2 eggs, beaten

1 c. milk
1 t. vanilla
1/2 c. oil
2 c. fresh raspberries

In a large bowl, mix flour, sugar, baking powder and salt; set aside. In a small bowl, blend eggs, milk, vanilla and oil together. Add egg mixture to dry ingredients, stirring until just moistened. Fold in raspberries. Place in lightly greased or paper-lined muffin tins. Bake at 350 degrees for 25 minutes or until nicely browned. Makes 24 muffins.

Create a tree just for your children...use fun
themes like Teddy bears, a dolls' tea party
or their favorite sport!

# Sour Cream Breakfast Coffeecake

*Mary Dungan*
*Gardenville, PA*

*My mom was busy with laundry, cooking, baking, canning and freezing, but she always had time for family, friends and neighbors. This is one of her best recipes.*

1 c. sugar
1 c. shortening
3 eggs, beaten
1 t. vanilla
2-1/4 c. all-purpose flour, sifted
1 t. baking soda

3 t. baking powder
1 c. sour cream
2/3 c. brown sugar
1-1/2 t. cinnamon
1/2 c. nuts, chopped

Cream sugar and shortening together. Add eggs and vanilla. Mix in flour, baking soda, baking powder and sour cream. Spread batter into a greased and floured tube pan. Mix together brown sugar, cinnamon and nuts. Spread on top of batter in pan. Bake at 375 degrees for 30 minutes.

Still-warm coffeecake makes a welcome gift! Tuck it in a round basket lined with cheery red fabric. Trim the edge of the basket with greenery, cinnamon sticks, bay leaves and sprigs of berries. Tie your gift card to the handle with several strands of raffia.

## Colorado Cocoa

Pat Akers
Stanton, CA

*Serve in jumbo mugs with whipped cream and a dash of cinnamon!*

3 T. cocoa
2 T. sugar
4 c. milk

3 T. semi-sweet chocolate, shaved

In a saucepan, mix together cocoa and sugar then pour in cold milk. Stir until sugar is well blended. Heat milk and shaved chocolate, stirring constantly with a wooden spoon, until milk is almost at the boiling point and chocolate is melted. Do not let milk boil.

To create a rustic tree with natural charm, begin with a grapevine garland. Soak several lengths of grapevine in warm water until pliable. Begin at the top and gently wrap the grapevine around your Christmas tree.

# Old-Fashioned Russian Tea

*Jeannie Craig*
*Charlotte, NC*

*My sister, brother and I always went to our Grandmother's house after school on Friday. If the weather was cool, we knew there would be a pot of Russian tea simmering on the stove. Grandmother always served it in a china cup and saucer which made it even more special. We felt so grown up sipping the tea from a china cup!*

juice of 4 oranges
juice of 4 lemons
1 c. water

3/4 c. sugar
3 pts. hot tea
1 t. whole cloves

Boil orange juice, lemon juice, water and sugar until sugar dissolves. Add hot tea and cloves. Simmer until ready to serve.

Decorations for your mantel can easily be made in minutes! Polish bright red apples with a soft cloth, core out the middles and fill with votive candles. You can do the same with green apples, artichokes, oranges, lemons or tangerines.

## Stuffed French Toast

*Debby Horton*
*Cincinnati, OH*

*It wouldn't be Christmas morning without this favorite breakfast dish. I make this the day before, then on Christmas morning, I serve a warm and cozy breakfast to enjoy in front of the fire and lighted tree.*

8 or more slices of hearty bread, crusts trimmed, cubed
2 8-oz. pkgs. cream cheese, cubed

12 eggs
2 c. milk
1/3 c. maple syrup

Place half of bread cubes in a 13"x9" pan. Top with cream cheese and layer on remaining bread cubes. Whip eggs; add milk and syrup. Blend well. Pour over bread and cheese. Cover dish with plastic wrap and refrigerate overnight. Next day, remove plastic wrap and bake at 375 degrees for 45 minutes or until nicely browned. Top with powdered sugar, syrup or any other of your favorite toppings.

Lighting your home each holiday with candles creates a cozy welcome. This year, gather all your favorite things and create new ways to display your candles. Tuck no-drip tapers into an old canning jar filled with buttons or scatter tea lights on plates set on a wire plate-stacker.

## Baked Peach Pancakes

*Mary Murray*
*Gooseberry Patch*

*Serve this warm, right from the oven, with slices of crisp bacon.*

2 c. fresh peaches, peeled and
    sliced
4 t. sugar
1 t. lemon juice
3 eggs
1/2 c. all-purpose flour

1/2 c. milk
1/2 t. salt
2 T. butter
nutmeg
sour cream

Combine peaches with sugar and lemon juice; set aside. In a mixing bowl, beat eggs until fluffy. Add flour, milk and salt, continue to beat until smooth. Place butter in a 10-inch oven-proof skillet and bake at 400 degrees for 3 to 5 minutes or until melted. Pour batter into hot skillet and bake for 20 to 25 minutes or until pancake has risen. Remove from oven, top with peach slices and sprinkle with nutmeg. Serve immediately with sour cream. Makes 4 to 6 servings.

Hang oversize mittens on your mantel instead
of stockings! Fill them with lots of goodies...
ribbon candy, movie tickets and popcorn balls.

## Raspberry Coffeecake

*Janet Myers*
*Reading, PA*

*This is my favorite coffee cake. It looks fancy, but is very easy to make. I'll never forget the time I took it to an auction and people kept bidding on it...if they only knew it was a biscuit mix!*

3-oz. pkg. cream cheese
4 T. butter
2 c. biscuit mix
1/3 c. plus 1 to 2 T. milk,
    divided

1/2 c. raspberry preserves
1 c. powdered sugar, sifted
1/2 t. vanilla extract

Cut cream cheese and butter into biscuit mix until crumbly. Blend in 1/3 cup of milk. Turn onto floured surface; knead 8 to 10 strokes. On wax paper, roll dough to 12"x8" rectangle. Turn onto greased baking sheet; remove paper. Spread preserves down the center of dough. Make 2-1/2 inch cuts at one-inch intervals on long sides. Fold strips over filling. Bake in a 425 degree oven for 12 to 15 minutes. Combine sugar, remaining milk and vanilla; drizzle on top.

Set a pair of vintage wooden skis by your door and secure them together. Wire a bundle of greenery in the middle, then tie on a pair of colorful mittens. Tuck sprigs of holly or mistletoe inside the mittens, letting some spill over the top.

## Country Scramble

*Dorothy Foor*
*Jeromesville, OH*

*All of our family's favorite breakfast foods in one casserole!*

2 c. frozen hash browns
1 c. fully cooked ham, chopped
1/2 c. onion, chopped
6 eggs, beaten

salt and pepper, to taste
1 c. Cheddar cheese, shredded
Garnish: fresh chives, minced

In a large skillet, sauté hash browns, ham and onion for 10 minutes or until hash browns are tender. In a small bowl, combine eggs, salt and pepper. Add to hash brown mixture and cook, stirring occasionally, until eggs are set. Remove from heat and gently stir in cheese. Spoon onto serving platter; sprinkle with chives.

*Christmas Eve, after I had hung my stocking, I lay awake a long time, pretending to be asleep and keeping alert to see what Santa Claus would do when he came.*

*—Helen Keller*

# Hearty Farmhouse Breakfasts

## Egg & Sausage Bake

*Joanne West*
*Beavercreek, OH*

*Make this on Christmas Eve, then you can enjoy all the fun on Christmas morning.*

12 slices white bread, crusts
   trimmed, cubed
1-1/2 lbs. bulk pork sausage
1/3 c. onion, chopped
1/4 c. green pepper, chopped
2-oz. jar chopped pimentos,
   drained

6 eggs
3 c. milk
2 t. Worcestershire sauce
1 t. dry mustard
1/2 t. salt
1/4 t. pepper
1/4 t. dried oregano

Line greased 13"x9" pan with bread cubes; set aside. In a skillet, brown sausage with the onion and green pepper; drain. Stir in pimentos; sprinkle over bread. In a bowl, beat eggs, milk, Worcestershire sauce, mustard, salt, pepper and oregano. Pour over sausage mixture. Cover and refrigerate overnight. Bake, covered, at 325 degrees for one hour and 20 minutes or until a knife inserted near the center comes out clean. Let stand 10 minutes before serving. Yields 12 to 15 servings.

String small nutmeg graters on a set of white lights
for your kitchen garland!

## Warm Country Waffles

*Betty Richer*
*Grand Junction, CO*

*Serve with warm peach slices with a bit of cinnamon and brown sugar. A dollop of whipped cream tops it off!*

2 c. flour
5 t. baking powder
1 t. salt

2 c. milk
4 eggs, separated
3/4 c. butter, melted

Mix dry ingredients together. Add milk, yolks and butter. Beat whites and fold into batter. Do not use electric beater for batter. Bake in a moderately hot waffle iron 4 to 5 minutes until crisp and brown.

## Cinnamon, Pecan & Honey Syrup

*Flo Burtnett*
*Gage, OK*

*In our family, my husband always makes the pancakes and waffles!*

2 c. maple syrup
1/2 c. honey

3/4 c. pecans, chopped
1/2 t. cinnamon

Combine all ingredients; stir well. Pour mixture into an airtight container. Store at room temperature. Serve over waffles or pancakes. Makes 3 cups.

# Brown Sugar Ham Balls

*Betty McKay*
*Harmony, MN*

*An easy-to-make favorite for your holiday open house!*

1 lb. ham
1/2 lb. beef
1 lb. lean pork
2 eggs, beaten
1/8 t. pepper
3/4 c. fine bread crumbs

3/4 c. milk
8-oz. can crushed pineapple
1/2 t. dry mustard
1/2 c. brown sugar
1/4 c. vinegar

Using a grinder, grind ham, beef and pork together 2 times. In a medium bowl, blend eggs, pepper, bread crumbs and milk together, add meat mixture. Shape into balls and arrange in a single layer cake pan. Mix together remaining ingredients and pour over ham balls. Cover with foil and bake at 350 degrees for one hour. Uncover and bake an additional 30 minutes.

Kids can make a clever chalk board gift bag for their teachers in no time! Have them write their holiday greeting with white paint on a black gift bag. Tuck the gift inside, fold the top over and punch two holes in the middle. Slip a pencil through the holes to secure the top of the bag!

## Dried Beef Spread

*Carol Sheets
Gooseberry Patch*

*Our family enjoys this tasty spread throughout the holidays; it's great for family get-togethers, caroling parties or church socials.*

8-oz. pkg. cream cheese
1/2 c. sour cream
2-1/2 oz. pkg. dried beef, cut
    into small pieces
2 T. milk

2 T. onion, minced
1/8 t. pepper
1/4 c. nuts
2 T. green pepper, chopped

Mix all ingredients together and spread in a pie pan or baking dish. Bake at 325 degrees until heated through. Serve warm with crackers.

A basket of greenery on the seat of an old rocking chair, a sled leaning against the rail and a pint-size evergreen in a child's red wagon... a pretty winter welcome for your porch!

# Cream Cheese Pastry

*Jan Sofranko*
*Malta, IL*

*Living on a sheep farm, we try to have interesting meals other than roasts and potatoes...here's one of our favorite appetizers.*

1/2 tube, 8-count crescent rolls
8-oz. pkg. cream cheese

1 T. dried dill weed
1 egg white

Unroll crescent roll dough and press seams together to form a rectangle. Pat all sides of cream cheese block with dill weed. Wrap cream cheese block in crescent roll dough; sealing edges. Set on a baking pan and brush with egg white and bake at 350 degrees for 20 to 30 minutes or until lightly browned. Serve with crackers.

# Garlic Dip

*Julianne Carlson*
*Mount Vernon, OH*

*I served this dip at a holiday candle party, and everyone wanted the recipe before they left!*

2 8-oz. pkgs. cream cheese
2 T. dill weed
1/2 t. salt
1/2 t. pepper
1 t. dried onion

1/4 onion, chopped
2 to 4 cloves garlic, minced
1 carrot, finely chopped
1 stalk celery, finely chopped
Garnish: paprika

Combine all ingredients, blending well. Sprinkle with paprika. Refrigerate overnight; soften 3 hours before serving. Serve with crackers.

# Home ♥ Style Beginnings

## Pine Cone Cheeseball

*Denise Bennett*
*Anderson, IN*

*This is a tasty and fun holiday cheeseball...your friends will be so impressed!*

8-oz. pkg. cream cheese
2 c. Cheddar cheese, finely shredded
1 bunch green onions, tops only, finely chopped

1/2 t. Worcestershire sauce
1/2 c. almonds, sliced

Blend cream cheese, Cheddar cheese, green onions and Worcestershire sauce in food processor until well combined. Place on serving dish. Shape into a cone shape and insert almonds vertically one at a time until cheeseball is completely covered and resembles a pine cone. Chill for 3 hours before serving to allow flavors to blend.

Help your children keep the spirit of Christmas...shovel a driveway or sidewalk for a neighbor, babysit for a busy mom or deliver goodies to a secret pal. Your children will learn that they benefit more than the receivers.

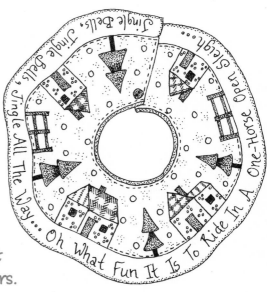

## Mixed Fruit Ball

*Jane Williams*
*Austin, MN*

*I like to make a pretty holiday presentation by surrounding this with clusters of red and green grapes and wedges of unpeeled apples.*

2 8-oz. pkgs. cream cheese,
  softened
1/4 lb. Cheddar cheese, grated
1 t. coriander
1/4 c. raisins, diced

1/4 c. dried apricots, diced
1/4 c. dried dates, diced
1/4 c. dried prunes, diced
1 c. pecans, chopped

Mix cream cheese, Cheddar cheese and coriander until well blended. Add dried fruits and stir gently. Shape into a ball and roll in pecans. Refrigerate overnight.

## Cream Cheese Fruit Dip

*Laurie Mounce*
*Houston, TX*

*Great served with a variety of fruit...tart Granny Smith apples, bananas and peaches are wonderful!*

8-oz. pkg. cream cheese
3/4 c. brown sugar
1 T. vanilla extract
1 c. peanuts

Blend together cream cheese, brown sugar and vanilla. Fold in peanuts. Chill well. Serve with your favorite fruit.

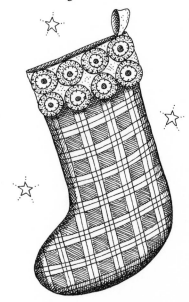

Happy, happy Christmas!
—Charles Dickens

# Home ♥ Style Beginnings

## Chicken Fingers & Honey Mustard
*Crystal Lappie*
*Worthington, OH*

*A tasty recipe you can make ahead of time! Prepare the honey mustard sauce up to 2 days before your holiday open house, and fry the chicken the day before...just wrap in foil and reheat!*

1/2 c. honey
1/4 c. Dijon mustard
4 4-oz. chicken breasts,
    skinless, boneless
1 c. all-purpose flour

1/2 t. salt
1/4 t. pepper
3/4 c. milk
1 c. vegetable oil

Blend honey and mustard in a small bowl. Set aside. Cut chicken into strips. Mix flour, salt and pepper in a small bowl. Place chicken in milk. Roll chicken strips in flour mixture until well coated. Pour 1/4-inch of oil into a large skillet. Heat over medium-high heat. Place chicken in an even layer in hot oil. Fry, turning once, for about 3 minutes on each side or until golden brown and crisp. Drain on paper towels. Serve with sauce.

*Share your favorite egg nog recipe in a decorative glass bottle. Don't forget to add a shaker of nutmeg!*

# Reuben Dip

*Jen Burnham*
*Delaware, OH*

*Add a basket of party rye slices or pumpernickel rye pretzels...*
*I guarantee it'll be a hit at your next party!*

16-oz. jar sauerkraut, drained
1/2 lb. deli-style corned beef,
   shredded
8-oz. pkg. cream cheese,
   softened

8-oz. pkg. shredded Swiss
   cheese
1/4 c. Thousand Island salad
   dressing

Combine all ingredients in a slow cooker. Cover and cook on high setting for 45 minutes, stirring occasionally, just until heated through and cheese is melted. Makes 6 to 7 cups.

Use a colorful quilt or length of red homespun
as a holiday tablecloth!

# HoMe ♥ STYLe BeGiNNiNgS

## Mom's BLT Dip

*Bonnie Neitzel*
*McFarland, WI*

*A family favorite for any get-together! Everyone will rave about how good it is and you'll be asked to share the recipe!*

2 c. mayonnaise
2 c. sour cream
4 tomatoes, diced

2 lbs. bacon, crisply cooked
and crumbled

Mix together mayonnaise and sour cream. Add tomatoes and bacon to the mixture. Refrigerate overnight for the best flavor. Serve with melba toast or rounds.

## Pepperoni Spread

*Deb Quaco*
*Wyndmoor, PA*

*Creamy and a little spicy...wonderful with sourdough!*

8-oz. pkg. cream cheese
10-oz. can cream of mushroom
soup

1/4 c. pepperoni, chopped
1 round loaf sourdough bread

Combine cream cheese, mushroom soup and pepperoni; blending well. Place in an oiled casserole dish and bake at 350 degrees until warm and bubbly; remove from oven. Hollow out center of sourdough bread and bake until crust is lightly crisp. Spoon warm dip in the hollowed-out sourdough round; serve with bread cubes or slices for dipping.

# Sweet Red Pepper Dip

*Liz Plotnick-Snay*
*Gooseberry Patch*

*Serve this with fresh vegetables and bagel chips.*

2 lg. red peppers
1 c. sour cream
2 3-oz. pkgs. cream cheese
3 to 4 roasted jalapeño peppers,
    seeded and chopped

1/4 t. salt
1/4 t. paprika
1/8 t. cayenne pepper

Cut red peppers in half lengthwise, remove stem and seed. Place peppers, cut side down, in a 8"x8" baking dish. Cover and microwave on high for 8 to 10 minutes, or until tender. Put peppers in cold water and remove skins. Dice peppers and combine remaining ingredients; mix well. Refrigerate 12 hours before serving.

Create a tree skirt to treasure. Lightly brush your children's hands with water-soluble paint and have them gently press their handprints onto a length of unbleached muslin. Use a permanent marker to add their names and the year. Tiny baby hand and foot prints would be darling, too!

## Cheryl's Holiday Cheese Ball

*Cheryl Kimball
Plymouth, MI*

*I don't remember where this recipe originally came from but, I have made it for almost every holiday gathering in my family. On the rare occasion that I don't make it, someone's sure to ask, "Where's that cheese ball Cheryl makes?"*

3 8-oz. pkg. cream cheese, room
   temperature
2 5-oz. jars blue cheese
1-1/2 t. garlic powder
1 lb. shaved ham, cubed

1 bunch green onions with tops,
   thinly sliced
1 sleeve round buttery crackers,
   crushed

Mix cream cheese and blue cheese with an electric mixer until creamy. Sprinkle in garlic powder, continue mixing. Add ham and green onions; blend thoroughly. Mixture will be soft. Cover and chill overnight, allowing flavors to blend. When ready to serve, place crushed crackers in a pie or cake pan. Spoon cheese mixture on top of the crackers and roll in crumbs. Serve with crackers.

# Santa Claus Milk

*Kathy Grashoff*
*Ft. Wayne, IN*

*A special treat for Santa...leave him a mug of this with a plate of snowflake-shaped cookies!*

4 c. plus 2 T. milk, divided
2-inch cinnamon stick
3 to 4 whole cloves

1/4 c. sugar
1 T. cornstarch
nutmeg

Combine 4 cups milk, cinnamon stick and cloves in a saucepan; cook over medium heat for 15 minutes, stirring occasionally. Do not boil. Remove from heat and discard spices. Combine sugar, cornstarch and 2 tablespoons milk; stir until smooth. Blend into hot milk mixture and cook one minute, stirring constantly. Pour into mugs and sprinkle with nutmeg. Makes 4 cups.

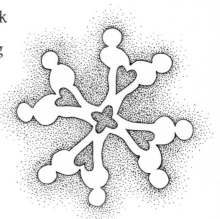

# White Christmas Punch

*Rebecca Boone*
*Olathe, KS*

*Add a sprinkle of freshly ground nutmeg on top!*

2 c. sugar
1 c. water
12-oz. can evaporated milk
1 T. almond extract

3 1/2-gal. cartons vanilla ice cream
6 2-ltr bottles lemon-lime carbonated drink

Combine sugar and water. Stir constantly, cook over medium heat until sugar dissolves. Remove from heat, add evaporated milk and almond extract; let cool. Chill until ready to serve. Combine milk mixture and remaining ingredients in punch bowl just before serving. Stir to break ice cream into small pieces.

# Home ♥ Style Beginnings

## Apple Creamy

*Coli Harrington*
*Delaware, OH*

*A spicy, winter warm-up!*

2 21-oz. cans apple pie filling
2 c. half-and-half
2 c. ginger ale
1 c. plus 2 T. apple cider, divided
1/2 c. brown sugar, firmly
  packed

1 t. apple pie spice
1 c. frozen non-dairy whipped
  topping, thawed

In an electric blender, blend pie filling until smooth. In a large saucepan, combine apple pie filling, half-and-half, ginger ale, one cup cider, brown sugar and apple pie spice. Mix well. Simmer over low heat until mixture is steamy, but do not boil. Mix whipped topping with remaining 2 tablespoons apple cider. Set aside.

### Streusel Topping:

2 T. brown sugar
2 T. sugar
2 T. walnuts, ground

1/2 t. cinnamon
1 T. butter, melted

In a small bowl, combine brown sugar, sugar, walnuts and cinnamon. Stir in butter; blend until mixture is crumbly. Pour apple creamy mixture into mugs. Top each serving with a dollop of whipped topping mixture and a sprinkling of streusel topping.

*Nestle a small artificial evergreen in an empty flour sack...perfect for the kitchen!*

# Hot Vanilla

*Vickie*

*A warm and creamy change from hot cocoa!*

| | |
|---|---|
| 1 c. milk | 1/8 t. vanilla extract |
| 1 t. honey | 1/8 t. cinnamon |

In a saucepan, heat milk until very hot but not boiling. Pour milk into a mug. Add honey, vanilla and cinnamon. Mix well and serve immediately. Makes one serving.

# Old-Fashioned Egg Nog

*Elena Tonkin*
*Powell, TN*

*This is my favorite because it represents the holiday season. My mother-in-law always serves egg nog during the holidays and everyone looks forward to it...we try not to overindulge!*

| | |
|---|---|
| 2 pasteurized eggs, well beaten | 1/4 t. salt |
| 14-oz. can sweetened condensed milk | 1 qt. milk |
| | 1/2 pt. heavy cream, whipped |
| 1 t. vanilla extract | nutmeg or cinnamon |

Combine eggs, sweetened condensed milk, vanilla and salt. Beat in milk. Fold in whipped cream; refrigerate until well chilled. Ladle into serving cups and dust with a sprinkling of nutmeg or cinnamon.

Create an evergreen swag then wire it to chair backs, top it off with a holiday bow!

# Home ♥ Style Beginnings

## Hot Mulled Punch

*Michelle Urdahl*
*Litchfield, MN*

*During the holiday season you will always find some of this punch brewing. It smells wonderful and tastes even better!*

1-1/2 qts. cranberry juice
2 qts. apple juice
1/2 c. brown sugar

1/2 t. salt
4 cinnamon sticks
1-1/2 t. whole cloves

Pour juices into 30 to 36-cup coffee maker. Place remaining ingredients in basket of coffee maker and brew according to coffee maker instructions. When complete, remove basket and discard spices. Serve hot. Makes 40 punch cup servings.

## Wassail

*Katheryn Kwiatkowski*
*St. Paul, NE*

*I remember being a new bride and being so nervous about my first Christmas Eve spent with my in-laws. The night was so cold and we hurried into my husband's family's home as it started to snow. My new mother-in-law greeted me with a big hug and a warm mug of her special wassail...I've loved both ever since.*

6-oz. can frozen orange juice
   concentrate
1 pt. hot tea
1 c. sugar

1 qt. water
2/3 c. pineapple juice
12-oz. bottle lemon-lime
   carbonated drink

Prepare orange juice according to package. In a saucepan, combine tea, sugar, water and pineapple juice. Just before serving, add lemon-lime drink. Makes 3-1/2 quarts.

# Baked Yams with Nutmeg Butter

*Jo Ann*

*Sweet brown sugar and nutmeg will make this side dish
a new favorite in your family.*

2 sticks unsalted butter, softened    1-1/2 t. nutmeg
1 c. brown sugar, firmly packed    12 yams

Using electric mixer, beat butter, brown sugar and nutmeg in medium bowl until light and fluffy. Preheat oven to 350 degrees. Line 2 large baking sheets with heavy-duty foil. Spray foil with non-stick vegetable oil spray. Using small sharp knife, make one slit in each yam. Place yams on baking sheets. Bake at 350 degrees 1-1/2 hours, or until yams are tender. Cut slits across center of each yam. Press ends toward center to expose flesh. Transfer yams to platter. Spoon one tablespoon nutmeg butter into each. Serve remaining butter to be added as desired.

Sort through your family's closets and donate "gently worn" and outgrown coats, clothes and extra blankets to a nearby shelter. They'll be much appreciated!

## Vanilla-Glazed Sweet Potatoes

*Teri Lindquist*
*Gurnee, IL*

*This heavenly dish is always on our holiday table! It is rich, delicious and there are never any leftovers!*

3 lbs. sweet potatoes, peeled
1/4 c. butter
1/4 c. light brown sugar, firmly
   packed
1 t. salt

1 t. orange zest, grated
1/4 t. black pepper
3 T. orange juice
1 T. vanilla extract
1/2 c. pecans, chopped

Boil sweet potatoes in water until tender; drain. Cool slightly, then cut into 1/4-inch slices. Arrange the slices in a greased, broiler-proof 13"x9" baking dish, overlapping slightly. In a small saucepan, melt butter over low heat. Add brown sugar, salt, orange zest, pepper, orange juice and vanilla; stirring until combined. Heat, but do not allow to boil. Remove from heat and brush sauce evenly over potato slices. Broil 6 inches from heat until golden, about 6 or 7 minutes. Sprinkle with pecans. Makes 6 servings.

Create snow-covered ornaments! Dip pine cones into white semi-gloss latex enamel paint. Insert an ornament hook in the top and hang to dry.
If you'd like a little extra sparkle, sprinkle white glitter over the paint before it dries.

# Christmas Cauliflower

*Jean Stokes*
*Ozark, AL*

*A cheesy dish that's great for holiday potlucks!*

1 lg. head cauliflower, broken
    into florets
1/4 c. green pepper, diced
8-oz. jar mushrooms, sliced and
    drained
1/4 c. butter

1/3 c. all-purpose flour
2 c. milk
4 oz. Swiss cheese, shredded
2 T. pimentos, diced
1 t. salt
Garnish: paprika

In a large saucepan, cook cauliflower in a small amount of water for 6 to 7 minutes or until crisp-tender; drain well. In a medium saucepan, sauté green peppers and mushrooms in butter for 2 minutes. Add flour; gradually stir in milk. Bring to a boil; boil for 2 minutes, stir in cheese until melted. Add pimentos and salt. Place half of the cauliflower in a greased 2-quart baking dish; top with half of the sauce. Repeat layers. Bake uncovered at 325 degrees for 25 minutes or until bubbly. Sprinkle with paprika. Makes 8 to 10 servings.

Float whole cranberries and pineapple slices
in your bowl of wassail.

## Golden Mashed Potatoes

*Donna Dye*
*London, OH*

*An old-fashioned dish from the heartland. Adding parsnips will give the potatoes just a hint of sweetness.*

1-1/2 lbs. Yukon Gold potatoes, peeled and cubed
1 lb. parsnips, peeled and cubed
1 lg. garlic clove, halved
3 c. water

14-1/2 oz. can chicken broth
1/4 c. whipping cream
1/4 stick butter
2 T. fresh parsley, minced
Garnish: fresh parsley, minced

Combine potatoes, parsnips and garlic in large saucepan. Add water and broth. If necessary, add additional water to cover potatoes. Boil uncovered for 25 minutes or until vegetables are tender. Drain vegetables, reserving liquid. Return vegetables to saucepan. Add cream and butter. Over low heat; mash until mixture is smooth and fluffy, adding enough reserved cooking liquid to thin to desired consistency. Mix in parsley. Transfer to serving dish. Garnish with additional parsley.

*A collection of pillar candles are pretty as a table centerpiece. Wrap tall ones with cinnamon sticks, secured with a wide homespun bow. Small chubby ones can be grouped in a stoneware pie plate.*

# Sourdough Bread Stuffing

*Mark Demidovich*
*Charleston, SC*

*Sourdough bread, bacon and mushrooms are a great
combination in this hearty stuffing.*

1-1/4 lb. sourdough bread,
   crusts trimmed, cubed
3/4 lb. bacon, crisply cooked and
   crumbled, drippings reserved
2 med. leeks, white and pale
   green part only, chopped
3 c. celery, chopped
1 lb. mushrooms, sliced

1-1/2 T. dried sage leaves
2 t. dried thyme
1 t. salt
3/4 t. black pepper
2-1/2 c. canned chicken broth
2 lg. eggs
1-1/2 t. baking powder

Preheat oven to 325 degrees. Spread bread cubes on 2 baking sheets.
Bake for 25 minutes or until bread cubes are dry and crisp, stirring
occasionally. Set aside. Prepare bacon, reserving 1/4 cup drippings.
Add leeks and celery to skillet and sauté in bacon drippings for
10 minutes or until tender and beginning to brown. Add mushrooms,
sage, thyme, salt and pepper; sauté for 10 minutes or until tender. Pour
mushroom mixture over bread cubes. Add bacon and toss to blend.

Mix in 2 cups of broth. Preheat
oven to 350 degrees. Butter
13"x9" glass baking dish.
Beat eggs and baking powder
together in a small bowl. Mix
eggs into stuffing; moisten
stuffing with more broth if it is
dry. Transfer to prepared baking
dish. Bake stuffing for one hour
or until cooked through and
golden brown on top.

## Grandma Margie's Scalloped Corn
*Crystal Lappie*
*Worthington, OH*

*My grandma always used a recipe but rarely ever followed it. I spent half of my time trying to remember how she made certain dishes and no matter how hard I tried I could never make the dish as tasty as she did. Years later I realized that it wasn't the recipe she used that made each dish so good but the patience and love she used to make each dish delicious and special. Someday I hope to pass Grandma's two special ingredients to my children so that they can cook with a little bit of love, too.*

10-oz. can corn, drained
10-oz. can cream-style corn
1 egg, beaten

1/3 c. milk
1 stick butter, softened
8-oz. box cornbread mix

Mix all the ingredients together; blending well. Spoon into a 2-quart casserole dish. Bake at 350 degrees for 45 minutes.

Let us keep Christmas still a shining thing.

—Grace Noll Crowell

# Potato & Spinach Casserole

*Barbara Bargdill*
*Gooseberry Patch*

*If you need a quick and delicious casserole for a family gathering or holiday potluck, this recipe is perfect!*

6 to 8 lg. potatoes, peeled,
    cooked and mashed
8 oz. sour cream
2 t. salt
1/4 t. pepper
2 T. chives, chopped

1/4 c. butter
10-oz. pkg. frozen spinach,
    thawed, drained and
    chopped
1 c. Cheddar cheese, shredded

In a large bowl, combine all ingredients except cheese. Spoon into a greased 2-quart casserole dish. Bake uncovered at 400 degrees for 15 minutes. Top with cheese and bake 5 minutes longer.

Make snow angels!

# Home ♥ Style Beginnings

## Baked Butternut Squash & Apples

*Joanne West*
*Beavercreek, OH*

*This is an old-fashioned recipe from the midwest;
the apples and maple syrup are wonderful together.*

2 med. butternut squash, peeled,
   and seeded
2-1/4 lbs. med. Granny Smith
   apples, peeled and cored
3/4 c. dried currants

nutmeg, freshly grated
salt and pepper, to taste
3/4 c. maple syrup
1/2 stick butter, cut into pieces
1-1/2 T. fresh lemon juice

Cut squash and apples crosswise into 1/4-inch slices. Preheat oven
to 350 degrees. Cook squash in large pot of boiling salted water for
3 minutes or until almost tender. Drain well. Combine squash, apples
and currants in 13"x9" glass baking dish. Season with desired amounts
of nutmeg, salt and pepper. Combine maple syrup, butter and lemon
juice in small saucepan. Whisk over low heat until butter melts. Pour
syrup over squash mixture and toss to
coat evenly. Bake until squash and
apples are very tender, stirring
occasionally; about one hour.
Cool 5 minutes.

String cranberries onto florist's
wire, then shape into a heart
or star.

# Farmstead Pumpkin Casserole

*Kathy Grashoff*
*Ft. Wayne, IN*

*My family always enjoys this traditional holiday dish...you can even use fresh pumpkins that you've grown!*

| | |
|---|---|
| 15-oz. can pumpkin | 1/2 c. sugar |
| 14-oz. can condensed milk | 4 eggs |
| 1/4 c. butter, melted | 2 t. cinnamon |

Preheat oven to 325 degrees. Mix all ingredients together in medium bowl. Pour into a 2-quart baking dish. Bake at 325 degrees 45 minutes or until set. Makes 6 to 8 servings.

A collection of Santas looks wonderful on the shelves of a pie safe...add lots of tiny votives to cast a soft glow. Fold a red and white quilt over one of the open pie safe doors or hang stockings from a length of twine.

## Pilgrim Sauce

*Barbara Etzweiler*
*Millersburg, PA*

*A long-time favorite at our home.*

1 c. frozen cranberry juice
  concentrate, thawed
1/3 c. sugar
12-oz. pkg. fresh cranberries
1/2 c. dried cranberries

3 T. orange marmalade
2 T. orange juice
2 t. orange zest
1/4 t. allspice

Combine cranberry juice concentrate and sugar in saucepan. Boil, stirring constantly until sugar dissolves. Add fresh and dried cranberries and cook for about 7 minutes or until fresh berries pop and dried berries soften. Remove from heat, stir in orange marmalade, orange juice, orange zest and allspice. Chill until ready to serve.

Create a festive glow...wrap glass votive holders
in sheer red ribbon.

# Old-Fashioned Coleslaw

*Liz Plotnick*
*Gooseberry Patch*

*No family get-together would be complete without this favorite!*

1/2 c. white wine vinegar
1/2 c. sugar
2 t. dried oregano
1 med. head green cabbage,
   finely sliced

2 red bell peppers, chopped
2 carrots, peeled and grated
2 celery stalks, chopped
3/4 c. red onion, chopped
salt and pepper, to taste

Combine vinegar, sugar and oregano in large bowl; stir until sugar dissolves. Add cabbage, bell peppers, carrots, celery and onion. Toss to combine. Season to taste with salt and pepper. Cover and refrigerate 4 hours, tossing occasionally.

Line the steps of an open staircase with layers of fresh cedar sprigs and scented candles. You can also stencil on white lunch-size paper sacks, fill the sack partially with sand and set a votive inside.

## Marinated Carrot Salad

*Helen Murray*
*Piketon, OH*

*A time-saving recipe you prepare the night before.*

1 lb. carrots, sliced
1 c. celery, chopped
1/4 c. dried minced onion
1-1/2 t. celery seed
3/4 t. lemon zest, grated
1/2 t. ginger

1/8 t. paprika
1 c. sugar
1/2 c. vinegar
1/2 c. water
1/3 c. vegetable oil

Cook carrots in boiling salted water about 10 minutes or until tender-crisp; drain. Toss carrots with celery, onion, celery seed, lemon zest, ginger and paprika. Combine remaining ingredients in a small saucepan; bring to a boil, stirring often. Pour over vegetables. Cover and chill overnight.

Make your holiday table really special! Create a simple centerpiece from a circle of mistletoe loosely wrapped in ribbon; nestle a pillar candle in the middle. Set tiny topiary trees at individual place settings and wrap napkins with twine; tuck in holly berries.

# Creamy Broccoli & Cauliflower Salad

*Judy Kelly*
*St. Charles, MO*

*You can also add any of your favorites to this salad,*
*try raisins, grapes, dried cranberries or bacon.*

1 c. mayonnaise
8 oz. sour cream
1/2 t. dried parsley flakes
1/2 t. dried dill weed
1/2 t. onion salt
1/2 t. seasoned salt
1 bunch broccoli, washed and
    broken into florets

1 head cauliflower, washed and
    broken into florets
2 eggs, hard-boiled, coarsely
    chopped
10 ripe olives
2-oz. jar pimentos, chopped
1 sm. onion, chopped

Prepare dressing by combining first 6 ingredients; mix well and set
aside. Combine broccoli, cauliflower, eggs, olives, pimentos and onion
in a large bowl. Spoon dressing mixture over the top; toss gently to
coat. Refrigerate overnight. Makes 8 to 10 servings.

Use tiny cookie cutters to
cut shapes from orange
or lemon peels...
add to your
homemade
potpourri. They also
look pretty floating
in your favorite
holiday punch!

## Crunchy Salad with Dill Dressing

*Betty Stout*
*Worthington, OH*

*Festive and colorful, we always take this salad to family dinners.*

4 slices bacon, crisply cooked
  and crumbled
1/3 head romaine lettuce, torn
  into pieces
8 oz. cherry tomatoes, halved
1/2 med. cucumber, sliced
1 red onion, thinly sliced

1/2 sm. fennel bulb, thinly sliced
1/2 c. plain yogurt
3 T. fresh dill, chopped
2 T. white wine vinegar
1 t. lemon zest, grated
3/4 t. salt
1/4 t. pepper

In a serving bowl, combine bacon, lettuce, tomatoes, cucumber, onion and fennel. In a separate bowl, combine yogurt, dill, vinegar, lemon zest, salt and pepper. Pour dressing over salad; toss lightly to coat.

Light your walkway with white candles!

# Ambrosia Waldorf Salad

*Barbara Etzweiler*
*Millersburg, PA*

*This recipe was shared with us by a friend; now it's one*
*we always make and enjoy during the holidays.*

2 c. cranberries, halved
1/2 c. sugar
3 c. mini marshmallows
2 c. apples, unpeeled and diced
1 c. seedless grapes, halved

3/4 c. pecans, chopped
20-oz. can pineapple tidbits,
  drained
1 c. heavy cream, whipped
Garnish: shredded coconut

In a small bowl, combine cranberries and sugar. In a large bowl,
combine the marshmallows, apples, grapes, pecans and pineapple.
Add cranberries and mix well. Fold in whipped cream. Cover and chill.
Garnish with coconut before serving. Makes 12 to 14 servings.

# Dark Cherry Salad

*Jan Stafford*
*Chickamauga, GA*

*A colorful and delicious salad Mom always made when we*
*were growing up.*

14-1/2 oz. can dark sweet
  cherries
8-oz. can crushed pineapple
3-oz. pkg. cherry gelatin
3-oz. pkg. strawberry gelatin

8-oz. pkg. cream cheese
1 c. nuts, chopped
2 c. cola-flavored carbonated
  drink

Drain juice from cherries and pineapple into saucepan. Heat juices and
add gelatin. Stir until thoroughly dissolved; cool. Blend cream cheese
and beat into cooled gelatin. Add fruit and chopped nuts. Stir in cola-
flavored carbonated drink.

## Mandarin Orange Salad

*Teena Kellam*
*Diboll, TX*

*Quick and easy to prepare; it's best topped with fresh dressing you make yourself. You can even bottle the dressing in old-fashioned canning jars and share with friends.*

3 to 4 c. green or red loose leaf lettuce, torn into bite-size pieces
15-oz. can mandarin oranges, drained

1/2 c. walnut pieces, toasted
1/2 purple onion, sliced

Toss all ingredients together. Set aside.

### Raspberry Vinaigrette:

1-1/3 c. raspberry vinegar
1-1/3 c. seedless raspberry jam
1-1/2 T. coriander
2 t. salt
1 t. pepper
3 c. olive oil

Combine first 5 ingredients in an electric blender. Turn blender on high, gradually adding oil. Chill. Toss salad with dressing. Serve.

*Line your mantel with graters of different shapes and sizes, then tuck a votive inside each one.*

# Honey-Carrot Salad

*Ann Magner*
*New Port Richey, FL*

*This salad can be made a day ahead to allow the flavors to blend.*

4 med. carrots, shredded
3/4 c. pineapple, finely chopped
1/3 c. plain yogurt
2 T. fresh mint leaves, chopped
2 T. lemon juice

1 t. honey
1/2 t. cinnamon
1/4 t. cumin
1/2 head leaf lettuce, torn into
    bite-size pieces

Mix all ingredients except lettuce in a medium bowl. Cover and refrigerate at least 2 hours or until chilled. Serve on a bed of lettuce. Makes 6 servings.

Make a pine cone garland to hang across a doorway.

# Home ♥ Style Beginnings

## Mozzarella & Tomato Salad

*Becky Sykes*
*Gooseberry Patch*

*Serve this salad at room temperature...it's wonderful!*

2 oz. mozzarella cheese, thinly
    sliced
2 med. tomatoes, thinly sliced
1 T. red wine vinegar
1 t. olive oil

1/2 t. Dijon mustard
1/2 t. dried parsley
1/4 t. dried basil
1/4 t. sugar
1/8 t. pepper

Cut sliced cheese into pieces that are about half the size of the tomato slices. On a large plate, alternate slices of tomato and cheese. Arrange slices so that the top half of each tomato is not covered with cheese. Mix remaining ingredients and drizzle over layers before serving. Makes 4 servings.

Twisted stems of rosehips look lovely in a
handwoven basket.

# Sour Cream Potato Salad

*Gail Banasiak*
*Dayton, OH*

*You can easily double this recipe for a holiday progressive dinner.*

2 lbs. red potatoes, peeled
1/2 c. mayonnaise
1/2 c. sour cream
2 T. prepared horseradish
1 T. fresh parsley, chopped
1/2 t. salt

1/2 t. pepper
3 bacon strips, crisply cooked
　and crumbled
4 eggs, hard-boiled and chopped
2 green onions, sliced

Cook potatoes in salted boiling water for 20 minutes or until tender.
Drain and cool; cut into cubes. In a large bowl, combine mayonnaise,
sour cream, horseradish, parsley, salt and pepper; mix until smooth.
Stir in potatoes, bacon, eggs and onions. Cover and chill up to
24 hours. Makes 6 servings.

Hang dainty lady apples on your Christmas tree.

FireSide
Soups&Breads

# Grannie's Basil Soup

*Deanna Maraglia*
*Grass Valley, CA*

*A great soup for rainy weekends...it warms the soul.*

1/2 lb. Italian sausage
1 med. red onion, chopped
1 green bell pepper, chopped
1 red bell pepper, chopped
2 cloves fresh garlic, minced
1 bunch of fresh basil
3 15-oz. cans Italian stewed
   tomatoes

6-oz. can of tomato paste
3 c. water
1/4 c. brown sugar
salt and pepper, to taste
Garnish: croutons, mozzarella
   cheese, shredded

Brown the first 5 ingredients together in a skillet. Drain fat and set ingredients aside. In the same skillet, simmer basil, tomatoes, tomato paste, water, brown sugar, salt and pepper for 30 minutes. Stir in browned ingredients. Turn on oven broiler. Place soup into individual oven-proof stoneware bowls. Sprinkle croutons and cheese on top of soup. Place under broiler until cheese has melted.

# Fireside Soups & Breads

## Wash Day Stew

*Sandra Crook*
*Jacksonville, FL*

*I was raised in rural Alabama and we had no washing machine, the only appliances we owned were a stove and refrigerator. Grandmother would do wash every Monday by building a fire, filling the old black iron pot with water and lye soap, and we would boil the clothes clean. We would then rinse and hang them up to dry. When all the work was done, this stew would be ready for Grandpa and the hungry wash women.*

1-1/2 lb. stew beef
1/2 c. canned mixed vegetables
1 c. water
28-oz. can stewed tomatoes
1 T. salt

2 T. sugar
1/2 c. celery, sliced
1/2 c. onion, chopped
2 c. potatoes, diced
1 c. carrots, diced

Preheat oven to 250 degrees. Place all ingredients into a greased casserole dish with a cover and bake for 3 hours. Stir stew and bake for 3 hours more. Keep stew covered throughout cook time, adding additional water if needed.

*Sprigs of Queen Anne's lace look like snowflakes when tucked on a small tree.*

# Spinach-Chicken Noodle Soup

*Ann Magner*
*New Port Richey, FL*

*Enjoy a warm bowl of this old-fashioned favorite!*

4  14-1/4 oz. cans chicken broth
1 c. onions, chopped
1 c. carrots, sliced
2  10-1/2 oz. cans cream of
   chicken soup
10 oz. frozen, chopped spinach,
   thawed

4 c. chicken, skinned, cooked
   and chopped
2 c. med. egg noodles
1/2 t. salt
1/2 t. pepper

Combine broth, onions and carrots in Dutch oven. Bring to a boil. Cover, reduce heat; simmer for 15 minutes. Add remaining ingredients. Bring to a boil, reduce heat and simmer uncovered for 15 minutes.

Give an old-fashioned
hatbox filled with cookies
and jars of sweet jams and
jellies to a special friend.

# Fireside Soups & Breads

## Ham & Bean Soup

*Kathy Grashoff*
*Ft. Wayne, IN*

*Our family really enjoys this soup. It's always a welcome lunch after a chilly day in the stands watching football!*

1 c. dry navy beans, rinsed and drained
8 c. water, divided
2 stalks celery, sliced
2 med. carrots, sliced
1 lg. onion, chopped

3/4 c. fully cooked ham, cubed
1 t. instant chicken bouillon granules
1 t. thyme
2 bay leaves
1/4 t. pepper

In a large saucepan, combine beans and 4 cups of water. Bring to a boil, then reduce heat. Simmer uncovered for 2 minutes. Remove from heat. Cover and let stand for one hour. Drain and rinse beans. In the same pan, stir together beans, 4 cups of fresh water, celery, carrots, onion, ham, bouillon, thyme, bay leaves and pepper. Bring to a boil, reduce heat. Cover and simmer for 1-1/4 hours or until beans are tender. Discard bay leaves. Using a fork, slightly mash the beans against the side of the saucepan to slightly thicken soup. Makes 4 servings.

The only gift is a portion of thyself.
— Ralph Waldo Emerson

# Holiday Cloverleaf Rolls

*Kathy Schroeder*
*Riverside, CA*

*I usually double this recipe and freeze any extra rolls. These are great for breakfast, warmed in the microwave with homemade jam!*

4 to 5 c. all-purpose flour, divided
1/3 c. sugar
1 t. salt
2 pkgs. instant dry yeast

1/2 c. water
1/2 c. milk
1/2 c. butter, melted and divided
2 eggs

In large bowl, combine one cup of flour, sugar, salt and yeast. In medium saucepan over low heat, heat water, milk and 1/4 cup butter until very warm. With mixer at low speed, gradually pour liquid into dry ingredients. Increase speed to medium; beat 2 minutes, occasionally scraping bowl with rubber spatula. Beat in eggs and enough flour to make a thick batter. Continue beating 2 minutes, occasionally scraping bowl. With spoon, stir in enough additional flour to make a soft dough. Turn dough onto lightly floured surface and knead for 10 minutes or until dough is smooth and elastic. Shape dough into ball and place in a large greased bowl, turning over so that top of dough is greased. Cover with towel; let rise in warm place, away from drafts, for one hour or until doubled. Punch down dough by pushing down the center of dough, then push edges of dough into center. Turn dough onto lightly floured surface; cut in half. Cover with towel for 15 minutes. Grease 24, 2 to 3-inch muffin pan cups. With sharp knife or kitchen shears, cut one-half of dough into 36 equal pieces. Shape each piece into a smooth ball. Place 3 balls into each muffin pan cup. Brush tops with remaining melted butter. Cover with towel; let rise in warm place for 45 minutes or until doubled. Repeat with second half of dough. Preheat oven to 400 degrees. Remove towel from rolls and bake rolls 10 to 15 minutes or until golden. Remove from pan. Makes 24 rolls.

## Wild Rice Soup
*Jo Ann*

*So thick and hearty, you could serve it as a main dish.
It's wonderful after a wintry day of shopping!*

3 c. wild rice, cooked
2 c. chicken, cooked and cubed
1 c. ham, cooked and cubed
2 med. carrots, shredded
2 stalks celery, sliced
4 c. half-and-half

1-1/4 c. chicken broth
1 med. onion, chopped
1/2 t. salt
1/4 t. pepper
1/4 c. all-purpose flour
3 T. butter, melted

In Dutch oven, combine all ingredients except flour and butter. Cook over medium heat, stirring occasionally, for 15 to 20 minutes or until heated through. In small bowl, stir together flour and butter; stir into hot soup. Continue cooking, stirring occasionally for 10 to 15 minutes or until thickened. Serves 6 to 8.

Hang a cheerful wreath on your barn door or gate!

# Bean & Pasta Soup

*Sandy Spayer*
*Jeromesville, OH*

*Fill several insulated containers with this terrific soup and hitch up the wagon for a winter hayride!*

2 T. olive oil
2 med. zucchini, cut in half
  lengthwise and thickly sliced
1/2 t. dried basil leaves, crushed
1/4 t. garlic powder
2  10-1/2 oz. cans condensed
  chicken broth
16-oz. can tomatoes, undrained
  and chopped

1/2 c. dry elbow or twist
  macaroni
15-oz. can kidney beans, rinsed
  and drained
Garnish: Parmesan cheese,
  grated

Over medium heat, heat oil in 4-quart saucepan. Add zucchini, basil and garlic powder and cook until vegetables are crisp-tender. Add broth, one soup can full of water and undrained tomatoes. Heat to boiling. Add macaroni. Reduce heat to low. Cook 10 minutes or until macaroni is tender; stirring occasionally. Add beans. Heat through, stirring occasionally. Sprinkle with cheese and serve.

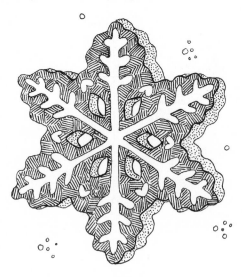

Send your holiday
guests home with
a jar of your
homemade preserves.

## Oatmeal Molasses Bread                                    *Vickie*

*An old-fashioned bread, we love it topped with apple butter!*

1-1/2 c. boiling water
1 c. long cooking oats
2 T. shortening
2 t. salt
1/4-oz. pkg. active dry yeast
3/4 c. warm water

1/2 t. sugar
1/4 c. brown sugar, packed
1/4 c. molasses
4-3/4 to 5-1/4 c. all-purpose
   flour
1 T. butter, melted

In a bowl, combine the first 4 ingredients; cool. In a mixing bowl, dissolve yeast in warm water. Sprinkle with sugar. Add oat mixture, brown sugar, molasses and 3 cups flour; mix well. Add enough remaining flour to form a soft dough. Turn onto a floured surface and knead for 6 to 8 minutes or until smooth and elastic. Place into a greased bowl; turn once to grease top. Cover and let rise in a warm place until doubled, about one hour. Punch dough down. Divide in half; shape into loaves. Place in 2 greased 9"x5" loaf pans. Cover and let rise for 30 to 45 minutes or until doubled. Bake at 375 degrees for 30 to 35 minutes or until golden brown. Remove from pans and cool on wire racks. Brush with butter. Makes 2 loaves.

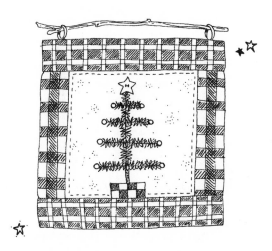

## Grandma's Chili

*Cheryl Waite*
*DeKalb, IL*

*I really like this recipe because the added bacon makes a wonderful change from other chili recipes!*

4 slices of bacon, crisply cooked and crumbled, drippings reserved
1-1/2 lbs. ground beef,
1 lg. onion, chopped
1/2 c. green pepper, chopped
3 lg. tomatoes
2 t. sugar
1 t. salt
1/2 t. pepper
1 garlic clove, minced
1 T. chili powder
15-oz. can tomato sauce
2 1-lb. cans kidney or black beans
Garnish: sour cream, shredded Cheddar cheese

In a large saucepan, prepare bacon, set aside. Cook ground beef in bacon drippings, add bacon to saucepan. Mix in all remaining ingredients except beans. Cook slowly for one hour. Add beans and cook 20 minutes longer. Garnish as desired.

Tie a festive holiday wreath to the front grill of your car or truck. A cheerful traveler's greeting!

## Carrot & Potato Soup

*Pat Woods*
*Syracuse, NY*

*I have been making this soup for over 30 years. My mother made it for us when we were young, as her mother did for her. I especially like to make this on a cold, wintry day.*

6 c. water
1 onion, chopped
4 carrots, sliced
5 potatoes, diced

12-oz. can evaporated milk
1/2 stick of butter
salt and pepper, to taste

In a saucepan, combine water, onion and carrots, simmer until crisptender. Add potatoes, cook until tender. Blend in evaporated milk and butter. Continue to cook for one minute over medium heat. Salt and pepper to taste.

For a sweet-smelling table decoration, hollow out a grapefruit half and tuck a votive candle in the center; surround the votive with cranberries. Place three or four surrounded with bunches of greenery on your sideboard.

# Honeybee Rolls

*Mark Demidovich*
*Charleston, SC*

*This roll has a slightly sweet taste; enjoy it with cinnamon butter!*

4 c. milk
3/4 c. margarine
1/2 c. sugar
1/2 c. honey
2 pkgs. active dry yeast

1/4 c. warm water
1/8 t. nutmeg
10 to 12 c. all-purpose flour,
    divided

In a saucepan, scald milk. Stir in margarine, sugar and honey; stir until sugar is thoroughly dissolved and cool to lukewarm. Dissolve yeast in warm water and add to milk mixture. Stir in nutmeg and 6 cups of flour. Add 4 to 6 cups of remaining flour, one cup at a time, until dough is no longer sticky. Knead dough on a floured surface for 5 minutes. Place dough in a well-oiled bowl, turning once to coat all sides. Cover and let rise until double in size. Punch dough down and divide into halves. Shape into rolls and divide among 4 oiled pie plates. Cover and let rise until double in size. Uncover and bake at 350 degrees for 20 minutes. Makes 4 dozen rolls.

Use children's toys to decorate...blocks, trains,
Teddy bears, dolls and wagons.

# Fíreside Soups & Breads

## Winter Chicken Stew

*Mary Turner*
*Montrose, CO*

*My kids' favorite recipe! A yummy way to warm up.*

1 roasting chicken
4 qts. water
2 t. salt, divided
1 c. celery, sliced
1 onion, diced
3 carrots, peeled and sliced
3 tomatoes, peeled and chopped
2 T. fresh parsley, chopped
6-oz. can tomato paste
1 t. dried oregano
1 t. dried basil
16-oz. can dark red kidney
    beans

15-oz. can garbanzo beans
16-oz. can baked beans
10-oz. pkg. frozen spinach,
    thawed and chopped
3 zucchini, sliced
1 lb. sweet Italian sausage,
    sliced
16-oz. pkg. homemade-style
    noodles
Garnish: Parmesan cheese,
    grated

Place chicken in a Dutch oven, cover with water add one teaspoon salt. Cover and simmer for 2 to 3 hours or until chicken easily falls off of the bone. Remove from the Dutch oven and separate meat from bones. Skim fat from broth. Return meat to Dutch oven, add celery, onion, carrots, tomatoes, parsley, tomato paste, spices, beans with liquid, spinach, zucchini and sausage. Simmer covered until vegetables and sausage are tender, approximately one hour. Cook noodles according to package directions. Rinse, drain and add to hot soup. Sprinkle each serving with Parmesan cheese.

I'm dreaming of a
white Christmas.

— Irving Berlin

# Cream of Fresh Tomato Soup

*Jocelyn Esber*
*Delaware, OH*

*A favorite of kids, big and little, everywhere! Who doesn't love this with a toasty grilled cheese sandwich?*

| | |
|---|---|
| 2 tomatoes, chopped | 1/8 t. pepper |
| 1/4 c. onion, chopped | 2 T. butter, melted |
| 1 sm. bay leaf | 2 T. all-purpose flour |
| 1/2 t. sugar | 2 c. milk |
| 1/2 t. plus 1/4 t. salt, divided | Garnish: green onion tops |

In saucepan, simmer tomatoes, onion, bay leaf, sugar, 1/2 teaspoon of salt and pepper for 10 minutes; strain and set aside. In same saucepan, add butter, stir in flour and add remaining salt. Blend in milk; cook over medium heat, stirring continually, until thick. Slowly stir in hot tomato mixture. Garnish with green onion tops. Makes 4 servings.

The holly's up, the house is bright, the tree is ready, the candles alight.
—Old German Carol

# Fireside Soups & Breads

## Sourdough Country Loaf

*Jeannine English*
*Wylie, TX*

*Every holiday table has room for a warm loaf of this*
*country   bread...everyone will want seconds!*

1/4 t. plus 2-1/2 t. active dry
   yeast
3 c. lukewarm water, divided
6 c. all-purpose flour, divided

1/2 c. semolina flour
1/4 c. whole wheat flour
2-1/2 t. salt

Prepare starter by dissolving 1/4 teaspoon yeast in one cup water. Add 2 cups all-purpose flour; mixture will be sticky. Let sit overnight on counter in a covered container. Container should be large enough for starter to grow. Dissolve remaining yeast in 2 cups water in a large bowl. Add one cup starter and let it sit for 10 minutes or until yeast foams. Gradually add remaining flours and salt. On a lightly floured surface knead for 10 minutes. Place dough into a well-oiled bowl and allow to rise for about 1-1/2 hours or until double in bulk. Turn dough onto a floured surface and cut into 2 balls. Roll each ball tightly. Cover with a damp cloth and let rise for 30 to 45 minutes. Preheat oven to 400 degrees. Place balls on a well oiled baking sheet. Slash the tops of bread balls with a very sharp knife. Remove damp towel and bake 35 to 40 minutes or until crust is golden brown. Leftover starter can be refrigerated one week.

Hang stockings on the backs of chairs!

# Brown Rice Turkey Soup

Tina Stidam
Delaware, OH

*Grandma's cold and flu remedy!*

| | |
|---|---|
| 2 carrots, thinly sliced | 3/4 c. brown rice, uncooked |
| 2 c. celery, diced | 1/4 c. dried parsley |
| 1 t. oil | 2 t. salt |
| 8 c. turkey stock | dash of pepper |
| 1 skinless turkey breast, boiled and cubed | |

Sauté carrots and celery in oil, until crisp-tender. Heat turkey stock to boiling. Add turkey and rice; simmer for 30 minutes, then add sautéed vegetables and seasonings. Simmer an additional 15 to 30 minutes.

Make a garland of all Christmas cards you receive;
they'll look festive if you hang it around doorways
or windows. Save the cards for next year; they'll
make wonderful gift tags.

# Fireside Soups & Breads

## Beef, Vegetable & Macaroni Soup

*Pam Vienneau*
*Derby, CT*

*My mother and grandmother made this soup on cold, snowy days,*
*served with homemade bread and jam!*

| | |
|---|---|
| 1 lb. stew beef, cubed | 1 bay leaf |
| 1 t. oil | 2 qts. water |
| 1 med. onion, diced | 4 carrots, peeled and sliced |
| 2 stalks celery, chopped | 14-1/2 oz. can cut green beans, |
| 1-lb. can stewed tomatoes, | drained |
| chopped | 1 c. macaroni, uncooked |

Brown stew beef in oil. Add onions and celery. Cook until tender. Blend in stewed tomatoes, bay leaf, water and carrots. Simmer for at least 2 hours. Stir in green beans and uncooked macaroni. Bring to a boil and cook for 20 minutes. Add water if mixture begins to boil dry.

Be sure your four-legged friends have a happy holiday, too! Hang a stocking for them filled with treats, chew toys and a brand new collar! If they spend lots of time outdoors, make sure to add a cozy blanket for them to snuggle up in and keep plenty of fresh food and water on hand.

# Butterhorn Rolls

*Francie Stutzman*
*Dalton, OH*

*These are the greatest!*

1 pkg. active dry yeast
1 T. plus 1/2 c. sugar, divided
1/4 c. plus 1 c. warm water,
   divided

1 c. butter, melted and divided
1 t. salt
3 eggs, beaten
5 c. all-purpose flour

Mix yeast and one tablespoon of sugar with 1/4 cup water and dissolve. Add one cup lukewarm water and 1/2 cup butter to yeast mixture, then combine with 1/2 cup of sugar, salt and eggs. Add flour, one cup at a time, mixing well. Cover and refrigerate overnight. Remove dough from refrigerator 3 hours before serving. Roll out in a circle, 1/8 inch thick and spread top with 1/4 cup melted butter. Cut in wedges like a pie. Roll each piece, starting at larger end. Place on greased cookie sheet, cover with a cloth and let rise in warm place. Remove cloth, brush with remaining melted butter. Bake at 375 degrees for 12 to 15 minutes.

Line an old pottery bowl with homespun, tuck in
some homemade sweets and tie on a bow.
Don't forget to include the recipe, too!

# Fireside Soups & Breads

## Beef & Barley Vegetable Soup

*Linda Charles*
*Delafield, WI*

*This homestyle soup is one of my favorites because it's healthy and it freezes well for later use.*

2-lb. soup bone with meat
2 T. oil
2 qt. water
1-1/2 t. salt
1/4 t. pepper
2 T. parsley, chopped

1/4 c. barley
1 c. carrots, chopped
1/4 c. onion, chopped
1/2 c. celery, chopped
2 c. tomatoes, cooked
1 c. peas

Remove meat from soup bone and cut meat into cubes. Brown lightly in oil. Place meat, soup bone, water, seasonings and parsley in Dutch oven. Cover tightly and simmer slowly for one hour. Add barley and simmer one hour longer. Cool and skim off excess fat. Remove soup bone. Add carrots, onion, celery and tomatoes. Simmer for 45 minutes. Add peas and continue to cook for an additional 15 minutes.

Give old-fashioned canning jars full
of your favorite, hearty soup.

# Hearty Vegetable Soup

*Cheryl Hambleton*
*Delaware, OH*

*Served with thick, crusty bread this soup makes a meal.*

2 T. olive oil
1 lg. onion, chopped
2 cloves garlic, minced
2 to 3 parsnips, peeled and
    thinly sliced
3 to 4 celery stalks, thinly sliced
3 carrots, thinly sliced
1 t. dried thyme leaves
1/2 c. wild rice, uncooked

1/2 c. whole barley
7 to 8 c. beef broth
2 c. water
3 to 4 sm. potatoes, peeled and
    cubed
1 tomato, peeled and diced
1 sm. bunch of fresh spinach,
    rinsed and trimmed
salt and pepper, to taste

In a Dutch oven heat oil over medium heat. Add the fresh vegetables and thyme. Cook, stirring frequently, until vegetables soften slightly. Rinse rice well and stir in with barley, broth, water, potatoes and tomato. Cover and bring to boiling. Reduce heat to medium-low. Cover and stir occasionally for one hour. Stir in spinach, salt and pepper. Simmer for 2 to 3 minutes longer.

*Close by the jolly fire I sit*
*to warm my frozen bones a bit.*

*— Robert Louis Stevenson*

## Granny's Biscuits

*Sandra Crook*
*Jacksonville, FL*

*I have used this recipe for many years and it has never failed.*
*It's a true "Southern biscuit!"*

| | |
|---|---|
| 4 c. self-rising flour | 1-1/2 c. buttermilk |
| 3 t. sugar | 1/2 c. vegetable oil |
| 3 t. baking powder | |

Preheat oven to 400 degrees. In large bowl, mix self-rising flour, sugar, and baking powder. Make a well in the center, pour in buttermilk and vegetable oil. Stir until blended. Shape dough and roll on a floured surface. Cut biscuits 1/2-inch thick. Place biscuits on an oiled baking sheet and bake at 400 degrees for 12 to 15 minutes.

Start a new tradition by sharing your Christmas cards at the dinner table. Set one at each individual place setting, then, one by one, have each member of your family read the greetings and letters aloud. You can even use them as holiday place cards!

# Old-Fashioned Chicken Soup

*Sandy Wisneski*
*Ripon, WI*

*This is a favorite in my family; it's very filling!*

2 whole chicken breasts
6 c. water
3 chicken bouillon cubes
6 peppercorns
3 whole cloves
14-1/2 oz. can chicken broth
10-3/4 oz. can cream of chicken
  soup

10-3/4 oz. can cream of
  mushroom soup
1-1/2 c. carrots, chopped
1/4 c. onion, chopped
1 c. potatoes, chopped
1 c. frozen peas, thawed and
  drained
1 t. seasoned salt

In a large stockpot, cook chicken in water with bouillon cubes, peppercorns and cloves until chicken is tender. Remove chicken from broth, bone and cube. Reserve broth and strain seasonings. Add chicken and mushroom soups, carrots, onion, potatoes, peas and seasoned salt back to broth. Cover and simmer soup on low until vegetables are tender.

## Dumplings:

2 eggs, beaten
1-1/2 c. flour
1/2 c. water

1/2 t. salt
1/2 t. baking powder
1/8 t. nutmeg

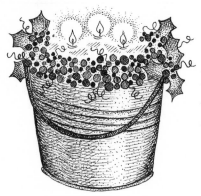

Mix ingredients well. Bring soup mixture to a boil and drop small amounts of dumpling mixture at a time into simmering soup. Reduce heat to a simmer and cook 10 minutes uncovered, cover and cook an additional 10 minutes.

# Fireside Soups & Breads

## Mamau's Biscuits

*Rebecca Chrisman*
*Citrus Heights, CA*

*When I was growing up, my grandmother kept a wooden bowl full of flour in the cupboard. She would pull that bowl out and start adding ingredients...before long she was cutting out biscuits with a jelly jar she used as her biscuit cutter. For me, the best way to eat these biscuits was to pour warm, sorghum molasses over butter, mix it up and dip the warm biscuits in the mixture.*

| | |
|---|---|
| 2 c. all-purpose flour | 1/3 c. vegetable shortening |
| 1 T. baking powder | 3/4 c. milk |
| 1 t. salt | |

Preheat oven to 425 degrees. Combine flour, baking powder and salt in bowl. Cut in shortening using a pastry blender to form coarse crumbs. Add milk. Mix with fork until dry mixture is moistened. Shape dough into ball. Put dough on lightly floured surface. Knead gently 8 to 10 times. Roll dough 1/2-inch thick. Cut with floured 2-inch round cutter. Place on ungreased cookie or baking sheet. Bake 12 to 14 minutes or until brown. Serve warm. Makes 12 to 16 biscuits.

Place a votive on an old butter paddle; add a few sprigs of greenery under the paddle and set it on a bench.

# Christmas Eve Sauerkraut Soup

*Judy Kelly*
*St. Charles, MO*

*This is a wonderful soup our family enjoys each Christmas Eve. Mom has altered the recipe over the years as our tastes have changed, but it has continued to be the main course at our family gathering.*

2 15-oz. cans Bavarian
   sauerkraut
8-oz. can mushrooms
2 qts. water

2 sticks butter, melted
1/2 c. all-purpose flour
3 c. half-and-half
salt and pepper, to taste

In blender or food processor combine undrained sauerkraut and mushrooms. Process until coarsely chopped. Put into large stockpot and add water. Bring to a boil and simmer for one hour. In large skillet, place butter and flour, stir over low heat until mixture is golden brown. Slowly add half-and-half until mixture is smooth. Add flour mixture to sauerkraut mixture. Keep soup on low heat while stirring in flour. Add salt and pepper, to taste. Let soup cool slightly before ladeling into a slow cooker. Read your cooker instructions for adding hot food to a cold slow cooker. Cook soup on low for 5 to 6 hours, stirring occasionally.

Turn your child's drawings into Christmas cards or notepads. So easy to do with a color copier. Grandma will love it!

# Fireside Soups & Breads

## Stew with Winter Vegetables

*Tammy Delfino*
*Attleboro, MA*

*A family favorite! It's packed full of hearty vegetables
and makes a terrific meal!*

5 c. water, divided
2 potatoes, cubed
2 carrots, peeled and sliced
1 lg. onion, chopped
2 T. beef bouillon granules
1 bay leaf
1-1/2 t. oregano
1 t. basil
1/2 t. pepper
1 egg, beaten
1/2 c. bread crumbs

1 t. minced dried onion
1 t. Worcestershire sauce
1/4 t. garlic salt
1/4 t. pepper
1 lb. ground beef
2 sweet potatoes, peeled and
   chopped
2 med. parsnips, peeled and
   chopped
1 c. frozen peas
1/3 c. all-purpose flour

In a large stockpot, bring 4-1/2 cups water to a boil. Add next
8 ingredients to stockpot, let water return to a boil, then reduce heat.
Cover and simmer 10 minutes. Prepare meatballs by combining next
7 ingredients, mixing well. Shape into 30,
one-inch balls; set aside. Add sweet potatoes
and parsnips to hot broth. Add meatballs,
one at a time and allow broth to come to
a boil. Reduce heat, cover stockpot and
simmer gently until vegetables are
tender and meatballs are thoroughly
cooked. Stir in frozen peas. In a small
bowl, combine flour and remaining
1/2 cup of water, blending well. Stir
into hot broth, and continue to cook
until mixture becomes thick
and bubbly.

# Never-Fail Dinner Rolls

*Elaine Crago*
*Gooseberry Patch*

*This recipe, given to our family by my aunt, is so easy and delicious!*

1 pkg. active dry yeast
1/4 c. lukewarm water
1/4 c. shortening
1-1/4 t. salt

2 T. sugar
1 c. boiling water
1 egg
3-1/2 c. all-purpose flour

Dissolve yeast in 1/4 cup water. Place shortening, salt and sugar in a separate bowl. Add boiling water to shortening mixture and stir until dissolved; cool. Add egg and dissolved yeast. Stir into flour; mix well. Place dough in large bowl. Cover and refrigerate. Chill 2 to 12 hours. Roll into a large circle and cut into 16 pie-shaped triangles. Beginning with the wide end of each piece of dough, roll and shape into crescents. Place on cookie sheet. Let rise until double in size; bake at 375 degrees for 15 minutes or until golden.

Bundle cinnamon sticks with ribbon and set in a basket near your fireplace...they'll soon scent the room.

## Mom's Chicken & Dressing

*Mary Ann Nemecek*
*Springfield, IL*

*I can remember my mother-in-law making this for large gatherings.
She would always double or triple the recipe because everyone
always requested seconds!*

all-purpose flour
4-lb. chicken, meat removed,
   cubed
8 c. bread, cubed
1-1/2 t. sage or poultry
   seasoning

1 sm. onion, chopped
1 stalk celery, chopped
4-oz. can mushrooms
10-3/4 oz. can cream of
   mushroom soup
10-1/2 oz. can of chicken gravy

Flour and brown chicken in skillet. In medium bowl, mix bread cubes,
seasoning, onion, celery, mushrooms and soup together. Place
browned chicken around outside of roaster. Place dressing in center
or on top of chicken. Spread chicken gravy on top of dressing. Cover
and bake for one hour at 350 degrees.

*Make a photo album for your children. Feature all the
wonderful things they've done the past year!*

# Cۤzy Kitchen Suppers

## Country-Style Ribs

*Crystal Lappie*
*Worthington, OH*

*This family recipe has been handed down for generations.*

3 to 4 lb. pork loin ribs
1 c. barbecue sauce
4-oz. can mushrooms

1/2 c. onion, chopped
1/2 c. green pepper, chopped

Place ribs in single layer on 13"x9" baking pan. Cover with foil and bake at 350 degrees for 1-1/2 hours. Drain off excess fat. Combine remaining ingredients and pour over ribs. Bake uncovered for 45 minutes, basting frequently with sauce. Serve with any additional sauce. Makes 4 to 6 servings.

Many merry Christmases, friendships, great accumulation of cheerful recollections, and affection on earth; heaven at last for all of us.

—Charles Dickens

# Nancy's Turkey Pie

*Delores Hollenbeck*
*Omaha, NE*

*While living in Germany, I often got together with a group of friends for lunch. When it was Nancy's turn to host lunch, she wanted to make this recipe...but the recipe was in storage in California! She called a friend living there who had the recipe and we're all glad that she did, it's great!*

| | |
|---|---|
| 1/2 c. butter, softened | 1 t. salt |
| 1 c. sour cream | 1 t. baking powder |
| 1 egg | 1/2 to 1 t. sage |
| 1 c. all-purpose flour | |

Combine butter, sour cream and egg. Beat at medium speed until smooth. Add flour, salt, baking powder and sage; blend at low speed. Mix well. Spread batter evenly over the bottom and up the sides of an ungreased 9" deep dish pie plate.

## Filling:

| | |
|---|---|
| 1/2 c. carrots, chopped | 2 c. turkey, chopped |
| 1/2 c. onion, chopped | 10-3/4 oz. can cream of cream |
| 1/2 c. green pepper, chopped |    of chicken soup |
| 1/2 c. celery, chopped | 1/2 to 1 c. Cheddar cheese, |
| 1/2 c. red pepper, chopped |    shredded |
| 2 T. butter | |

Mix together vegetables, butter, turkey and soup; place into pie crust and sprinkle with Cheddar cheese. Bake for 25 to 30 minutes in 400 degree oven. Let stand 10 minutes before serving.

# Cozy Kitchen Suppers

## Cabbage & Pork Chop Casserole

*Diane Long*
*Gooseberry Patch*

*An old-fashioned recipe, I usually don't even measure the ingredients,*
*I just keep adding them until it "looks right!"*

4 pork chops
1 T. oil
10-3/4 oz. can cream of celery
   soup

1/2 c. milk
1/2 head of cabbage, shredded
6 potatoes, sliced

Brown pork chops in oil, remove to plate. Add soup and milk to pork chop drippings, stirring well, bring to a simmer and cook until soup and milk are well-blended. Place cabbage on the bottom of a 13"x9" pan. Lay pork chops on top of cabbage. Layer potatoes over pork chops and pour soup mixture on top. Bake at 350 degrees for 1-1/2 hours or until pork chops are tender.

Create Christmas memories...take pictures, dress up, invite friends to visit, sing carols, make a snowman, watch all the old, classic Christmas movies and take a nap! Drop in to visit friends and relatives, it gives them a break from all the festivities and both of you a chance to catch up.

# Holiday Ham Loaf

*Roberta Clark*
*Delaware, OH*

*A "secret" recipe!*

| | |
|---|---|
| 2 T. onions, minced | 1/4 lb. ground ham |
| 3/4 c. bread crumbs | 3/4 lb. ground pork |
| 1 lg. egg | salt and pepper, to taste |
| 1/4 c. milk | 1/4 c. brown sugar |

Combine first 4 ingredients. Mix in ham, pork, salt and pepper and form into a loaf shape. Cover loaf with brown sugar and place in loaf pan. Cover with foil. Bake at 325 degrees for 1-3/4 to 2 hours. Uncover the last 20 minutes. Serves 5 to 6.

Be an elf...leave a present on someone's doorstep!

## Maple Roasted Chicken

*Jane Williams*
*Austin, MN*

*There is something really wonderful about the smell of maple and chicken. Serve it when the weather calls for something to warm the heart and tummy!*

7-lb. roasting chicken
salt and pepper, to taste
1 lg. onion, peeled and cut into
  wedges
1 med. butternut squash, peeled
  and cubed

6 carrots, peeled and cut in half
  lengthwise
3 parsnips, peeled and sliced
2/3 c. maple syrup
2 T. butter

Sprinkle the inside of the chicken with salt and pepper. Spread the vegetables in the bottom of a deep roasting pan and place the chicken on top. In small saucepan, over low heat, mix together syrup and butter until butter melts. Roast the chicken 2-1/2 to 3 hours, basting with the syrup and then the pan juices. Chicken is done when the breast is pierced and juices run clear. If chicken becomes too brown before cooking time is complete, cover loosely with foil. Remove chicken to a large platter, place vegetables around the edge of chicken. Serves 6.

A holiday keepsake; use a permanent marker to trace your children's hands on a solid color tablecloth. Have them write their names and ages with a pencil then embroider over the pencil lines. Gently wash to remove all pencil markings.

# Country-Fried Steak

*Sally Foor*
*Jeromesville, OH*

*This recipe brings back fond memories of visiting grandparents for supper. Everyone gathered around the table...it was a time to cherish family.*

3/4 c. plus 2 T. all-purpose flour, divided
1 t. salt, divided
1/2 t. pepper, divided
1/2 c. buttermilk

1 lb. beef cube steaks
1/4 c. plus 2 T. vegetable oil, divided
1 c. milk

Stir together 3/4 cup flour, 3/4 teaspoon salt and 1/4 teaspoon pepper in a shallow bowl. Coat steaks with flour mixture, then dip in buttermilk; coat again in flour. Heat 1/4 cup oil in a large skillet over medium heat. Add steaks and cook 5 minutes on each side. Remove from skillet and set aside. Heat remaining oil in skillet, stir in remaining flour. Whisk continually for 5 minutes or until golden. Gradually blend in milk, whisking continually, until thick, about 10 minutes. Stir in remaining salt and pepper, spoon over steaks. Serves 4.

Start a collection for someone special this year...Santas, snowmen, teacups or pottery. Add to their collection each year.

## Sunday Night Supper

*Robbin Chamberlain*
*Gooseberry Patch*

*Serve with homemade biscuits and warm cinnamon applesauce.*

2 T. butter, melted
1 lg. onion, finely chopped
1 lg. green pepper, finely
   chopped
1 med. potato, peeled and grated
6 to 8 eggs, slightly beaten

1 t. salt
1/2 t. thyme
1/4 t. pepper
1 lb. bulk sausage, cooked
   and crumbled
Garnish: paprika

Place butter in a large skillet, add vegetables and sauté until tender but not brown. In medium bowl, place eggs and add in seasonings; beat until frothy. Stir this mixture into skillet with vegetables. Cook over low heat stirring until eggs are set but still moist. Add sausage and stir into eggs. Sprinkle with paprika.

Cut an orange in half and scoop out the inside. Add a hole on each side and slip loops of raffia for hanging. Fill with birdseed for a winter treat.

# Chicken & Strudel

*Gena Pederson*
*Minot, ND*

*Gena's daughter, Donna Cozzens, shared this recipe with us, as well as her wonderful memory. "I can still see my mother stretching the strudel dough across her table until it was paper thin with barely a tear. We would all gather around to watch Mama, it was a real family event to see her at her best in the kitchen. What a delight it was for all of us to sit down together at the dining room table."*

3 c. all-purpose flour
1 t. salt
1-1/2 c. water
1 c. plus 1 T. shortening, heated,
   divided

1 fryer chicken, cut-up
salt and pepper, to taste

Mix flour, salt and water well; let stand for one hour. Spread enough heated shortening over dough to make it pliable. Save remaining shortening, keeping it warm to help with the stretching. Using your hands, stretch dough over a kitchen table. Continue to add shortening and stretch dough until paper thin. Roll up dough lengthwise, jelly roll style, until the dough is in the shape of a long string. Cut dough into 6-inch wide sections; set aside. In a stockpot, brown chicken in one tablespoon of shortening. Add salt and pepper. Add enough water to cover chicken. Bring to a boil, then reduce heat to simmer. Place the 6-inch rolls of dough on top of chicken in a circular pattern, until all dough is in the stockpot. Cover, simmer one hour.

*Ask your grandma to describe Christmas as it was when she was growing up.*

## Garden Meat Loaf

*Tina Stidam
Delaware, OH*

*This is so tasty; my sons love it!*

2 garlic cloves, pressed
1 sm. onion, finely chopped
2 celery stalks, finely chopped
1 lg. carrot, shredded
2 lbs. lean ground beef
1/2 c. quick-cooking oats

2 eggs
3/4 c. chili sauce, divided
2 t. dried thyme leaves
1 t. salt
1/4 t. ground black pepper

Preheat oven to 375 degrees. Place garlic into 2-quart batter bowl. Add onion, celery, carrot, ground beef, oats, eggs, 1/4 cup of chili sauce, thyme, salt and pepper. Mix lightly but thoroughly. Shape meat mixture into loaf in greased loaf pan. Bake one hour. Spoon the remaining 1/2 cup of chili sauce over meatloaf. Bake for an additional 10 minutes or until meat is no longer pink in center. Remove from oven. Let stand 10 minutes before slicing. Makes 8 servings.

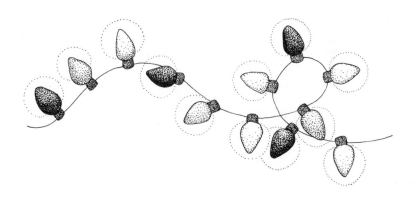

Hang a pair of ice skates on an old wooden sled.
Add some greenery and a holiday bow.

# Mom's Lasagna

*Julie Miller*
*Columbus, OH*

*This is the best I've ever had! Whenever I serve it, I've always
received requests for the recipe.*

1/4 lb. Italian sausage
3/4 to 1 lb. hamburger
1 clove garlic, minced
1 T. basil
1-1/2 t. salt
1-lb. can tomatoes, cut-up
12-oz. can tomato paste
12 strips lasagna noodles

3 c. ricotta cheese
1/2 c. Parmesan cheese, grated
2 T. parsley flakes
2 eggs, beaten
2 t. salt
1/2 t. pepper
1 lb. mozzarella cheese, grated

Brown sausage and hamburger. Spoon off excess fat and add garlic, basil, salt, tomatoes and tomato paste. Simmer for 30 minutes, stirring occasionally. Cook lasagna noodles in salted boiling water until tender. In medium bowl, combine ricotta cheese, Parmesan cheese, parsley, eggs, salt and pepper. Grease 13"x9" baking dish with vegetable oil. Place ingredients in pan in the following order: 1/3 meat, 3 noodles, 1/4 cheese mixture, 3 noodles, 1/4 cheese mixture, 1/3 meat, 1/2 mozzarella cheese, 3 noodles, 1/4 cheese mixture, 3 noodles, 1/4 cheese mixture,1/2 mozzarella cheese, 1/3 meat. Bake for 30 minutes at 375 degrees. Let stand 10 minutes before serving.

# Cozy Kitchen Suppers

## Brown Sugar Ham Steaks

*Kristi Warzocha*
*Lakewood, OH*

*Baking ham in milk is an Amish tradition; the ham will be
tender and faintly sweet in taste. We love it with mashed
potatoes and old-fashioned milk gravy!*

| | |
|---|---|
| 2 1-inch thick slices cured ham | 1 t. allspice |
| 1 t. dry mustard | 1/4 t. pepper |
| 5 T. brown sugar | 2 c. milk |

Place ham slices in a 13"x9" baking dish, sprinkle with mustard,
brown sugar, allspice and pepper. Add enough milk to just cover the
ham slices. Bake at 325 degrees for one hour. Continually check to
make sure milk is covering ham, add more milk if needed. When ham
is tender, remove from oven and cut into serving sizes.

Display all of your holiday
books in a basket by a
cozy chair. Set aside a night
to gather the family
around and read your
favorites together.

# Honey Roasted Pork Loin

*Sultana Purpora*
*Englewood, OH*

*A wonderful, old-fashioned main dish when served with homemade stuffing or noodles.*

2 to 3-lb. boneless pork
  loin roast
1/4 c. honey
2 T. Dijon mustard

2 T. mixed or black
  peppercorns, crushed
1/2 t. dried thyme
1/2 t. salt

Place roast on a lightly greased rack in a shallow roasting pan. Combine honey and next 4 ingredients; brush half of mixture over roast. Bake at 325 for one hour; brush with remaining honey mixture. Bake 30 additional minutes or until thermometer inserted in thickest portion registers 160 degrees.

Add greenery sprigs to lunch-size brown paper sacks, tuck in berries and display on your mantel.

## Country Chicken Pie

*Colleen Vasconcellos*
*Miami, FL*

*An easy and delicious recipe for leftover chicken;*
*add any of your favorite vegetables.*

2 pie crusts, unbaked
2 c. chicken, cooked
13-1/4 oz. can mixed vegetables
8-oz. can corn, drained
1 t. parsley

1 t. basil
2 c. milk
4 T. flour
salt and pepper, to taste
1 egg, lightly beaten

Preheat oven to 325 degrees. Place one crust in greased pie pan; add chicken and vegetables. In small saucepan bring next 5 ingredients to a boil, stirring constantly. Turn down to medium heat, stirring constantly until thick. Pour over vegetables and chicken. Cover with the second pie crust, and crimp edges to seal. Using a pastry brush, glaze the top crust with egg. Bake for 30 minutes or until browned.

Hang jingle bells from ribbons then tie
on your doorknobs!

# Oven Baked Barbecue Beef

*Corrine Lane*
*Marysville, OH*

*Whenever my Grandmother Mimi would come to visit from
Michigan, we knew that she'd bring this favorite dish.
Instead of cookies we wanted her barbecue beef!*

| | |
|---|---|
| 10-3/4 oz. can tomato soup | 2 T. Worcestershire sauce |
| 1/3 c. vinegar | 1 t. celery salt |
| 1 c. water | 1 t. garlic salt |
| 1/4 c. sugar | 2 lbs. stew beef |
| 1 sm. onion, diced | |

Preheat oven to 350 degrees. In a covered roasting pan, mix together
tomato soup, vinegar, water, sugar, onion, Worcestershire sauce, celery
salt and garlic salt. Add stew beef to the mixture. Cover and roast at
350 degrees for 2 hours. Remove from oven and mash with a potato
masher until stew beef is shredded. Cover and roast at 350 degrees for
one hour. Serve on hamburger buns.

Bring back childhood memories. Arrange a grouping of
well-loved stuffed animals, toys and children's books. Use
lots of fresh greenery and ribbons. Pile gifts in a little red
wagon, on a child's sled or tucked into a baby doll carriage.

## Peppered Sirloin Steak

*Kathie Stout*
*Worthington, OH*

*This quick and delicious dish only takes 15 minutes to cook!*

2-1/2 lb. sirloin steak
1/2 c. butter
1/4 c. fresh parsley
2 T. Worcestershire sauce

1/4 c. onion, minced
1 t. pepper
1/2 t. dry mustard

Preheat broiler. Lightly score edges of steak at one-inch intervals. Combine butter, parsley, Worcestershire sauce, onion, pepper and mustard in a small saucepan. Over low heat, stir mixture until butter melts; set aside 1/4 cup. Place steak on broiler pan and brush with butter mixture. Broil, basting often with butter mixture, approximately 6 minutes on each side of steak. Remove to a serving platter, slice across the grain and drizzle with reserved butter mixture.

Don't forget the cookies and milk for Santa!

# Homemade Chicken & Egg Noodles
*Michelle Urdahl*
*Litchfield, MN*

*This recipe was passed down to me by my grandmother. When I was little, she always let me cut the noodles into strips.*

2 t. salt
1-1/2 c. all-purpose flour
2 eggs
1 whole chicken

salt and pepper, to taste
Optional: 1/2 c. carrot, peeled and chopped, 1/2 c. celery, chopped

Mix salt, flour and eggs together. Roll out dough on large cutting board until very thin. Cut noodles in strips, using a sharp knife. Let slightly air dry on board. Add chicken to stockpot and add enough water to cover. Cook for approximately one hour or until done. Reserving broth, remove chicken from stockpot. Stir in vegetables, if using. Continue to simmer broth while removing meat from bone. Bring reserved broth to a boil, drop noodles in, stirring constantly. Reduce heat to simmer. Add chicken and cook until tender, approximately 20 minutes. Season with salt and pepper.

For somehow, not only at Christmas, but all the long year through, the joy that you give to others is the joy that comes back to you.

–John Greenleaf Whittier

## Stuffed Pepper Cups

*Crystal Cull*
*Montgomery, IL*

*This was my grandmother's recipe. She never had a recipe box, she would just write them down in a little notebook, mostly in pencil. I rewrote them and then filed them in a recipe box, but I still cherish her little notebook!*

6 to 7 med. green peppers,
    washed and seeded
2 lb. ground beef
1/2 c. onion, chopped
1 T. oil
2 c. tomatoes, stewed

3/4 c. rice, cooked
salt and pepper, to taste
2 T. Worcestershire sauce
1 c. sharp Cheddar cheese,
    shredded
1 T. steak sauce

Place peppers in a stockpot, add enough water to cover and cook approximately 5 minutes. Remove peppers from water and set aside. In a saucepan, brown beef and onions in hot oil, drain. Add tomatoes, rice, salt, pepper and Worcestershire sauce. Cover and simmer until rice is tender. Add cheese and steak sauce; stuff peppers. Place stuffed peppers in a 13"x9" baking dish. Bake at 350 degrees for 25 to 30 minutes.

Take a Christmas photograph of your family in the same place, same position each year...a record of how the kids have grown!

# Baked Ham in a Blanket

*Richard Welsch*
*Toledo, OH*

*While the ham is cooking the house fills with a wonderful aroma. That smell always meant celebrations at home. The spice blanket flavors the ham and keeps it moist. Yum! Any leftover ham makes great sandwiches the next day!*

| | |
|---|---|
| 2 c. all-purpose flour | 1 T. dry mustard |
| 1/2 c. brown sugar | 1/2 t. black pepper |
| 1 T. cloves | cider or water |
| 1 T. cinnamon | 5 to 6-lb. ham |

Make a spice dough by combining the flour, sugar and seasonings in a large mixing bowl. Add enough cider or water to make a rather stiff dough. Place the ham in a foil-lined open roasting pan, with the fat side up. Cover top and sides of the ham with a blanket of dough. Bake at 350 degrees for 3 hours. Remove ham and slice. Serve warm or cooled.

Take an annual Christmas hayride with friends
and family! Sing carols, visit neighbors and
bring lots of cocoa to share!

## Hearty Beef Brisket

*Joanne West*
*Beavercreek, OH*

*Slow-cooking makes the meat tender. Let it roast while
you wrap packages or trim the tree!*

16-oz. can stewed tomatoes,
   chopped
8-oz. can sauerkraut
1 c. applesauce

2 T. brown sugar
3-1/2 lb. beef brisket
2 T. cold water
2 T. cornstarch

Combine tomatoes, sauerkraut, applesauce and brown sugar in a Dutch oven. Bring to a boil, then reduce heat. Add brisket, spooning tomato mixture over top; cover and simmer on low 2 to 3 hours, or until meat is tender. When brisket is thoroughly cooked, remove from Dutch oven and set aside. In a small bowl, combine cold water and cornstarch, whisking well. Blend into tomato mixture in Dutch oven. Cook until mixture thickens, continue to cook for 2 minutes more. Spread sauce over top of brisket, reserving some as gravy.

Share saved flower seeds from
last summer with a special
gardening friend. Package
your gift in decorated
half-pint canning jars,
or slip the seed packets
in your greeting card.

# Sweet-and-Spicy Glazed Turkey                    *Vickie*

*Red pepper flakes kick up the brown sugar-orange glaze
that coats this turkey.*

1 c. orange juice
1/4 c. brown sugar, packed
2 T. butter
1 t. red pepper flakes
1 t. orange zest
1/4 t. salt
1/4 t. pepper
9- to 10-lb. turkey

1 orange, cut into 4 wedges
1 onion, cut into 4 wedges
2 T. butter, softened
1 t. salt
1/2 t. pepper
Optional: roasted Brussels
   sprouts

Combine first 7 ingredients in a medium saucepan; bring to a boil over
medium-high heat. Reduce heat and simmer 15 minutes or until
mixture is syrupy and reduced to about 2/3 cup. Set aside. Remove
giblets and neck from turkey; discard or refrigerate for another use.
Rinse turkey with cold water; pat dry with paper towels. Place turkey,
breast side up, on a lightly greased rack in an aluminum foil-lined
broiler pan. Lift wingtips up and over back and tuck under bird. Place
orange and onion wedges inside turkey cavity. Rub softened butter all
over outside of turkey, including legs. Tie ends of legs together with
heavy string. Sprinkle turkey all over with salt and black pepper. Bake,
uncovered, at 325 degrees for one hour. Brush turkey with half of the
glaze; bake, brushing with glaze every 30 minutes, 1-1/2 more hours
or until a meat thermometer inserted into meaty
part of thigh registers 170 degrees. Cover turkey
with aluminum foil during cooking, if necessary,
to prevent excessive browning. Transfer turkey to
a serving platter; cover turkey with foil and let
stand up to 30 minutes before carving. Garnish
with roasted Brussels sprouts, if desired.
Serves 9 to 10.

*Children's drawings make wonderful
note cards or stationery. It's easy
to have them printed and
grandparents will love them!*

Old-Fashioned Egg Nog, page 42

Stuffed French Toast, page 23

Homemade Chicken & Egg Noodles, page 106

Applesauce Pancakes, page 15

Old-Fashioned Spicy Pumpkin Pie, page 139

Cream of Fresh Tomato Soup, page 76

Hot Mulled Punch, page 43

Reuben Dip, page 36

Pork & Raspberry Sauce, page 112

Grandma's Chili, page 72

Ambrosia Waldorf Salad, page 58

Mom's BLT Dip, page 37

Sweet Red Pepper Dip, page 38

Mom's Lasagna, page 100

Grandma Margie's Scalloped Corn, page 49

Garden Meat Loaf, page 99

Beef & Barley Vegetable Soup, page 81

Roast Turkey & Gravy, page 110

Caramel Apple Crisp, page 138

Grandma's Blackberry Cobbler, page 120

Candy Cane Thumbprints, page 123

Molasses Gingersnap Cookies, page 141

## Chicken & Dumplings

*Joellen Crouch*
*Lower Lake, CA*

*Many of us would stand around the old wooden kitchen table and catch up on family news while we watched my tiny grandmother roll the dumplings with all her strength. Her dedication to their perfection often made me think that the health and happiness of all of us depended on her pot of chicken and dumplings.*

3 c. chicken, cooked and
   shredded
10-3/4 oz. can cream of
   chicken soup
2 15-oz. cans chicken broth
1/2 t. pepper
1 t. plus 1/8 t. salt, divided

1-1/2 c. all-purpose flour
1/4 t. baking powder
1/2 c. parsley leaves,
   coarsely torn
1 egg
1/4 c. cooking oil
milk

In a large saucepan, combine chicken, soup, broth, pepper and one teaspoon salt. Mix well, bring to a boil, reduce heat and simmer, covered. In large bowl, combine flour, baking powder, 1/8 teaspoon salt and parsley. Form a well in middle and add egg and oil; mix until very stiff. Add just enough milk for a stiff dough, mix with fork, then knead with hands. Divide dough in half. On floured surface, roll dough until very thin. Cut strips of dough one-inch wide by 2-inches long. Drop into simmering broth, stirring to separate dumplings. Repeat with remaining dough. Simmer until thick and noodles are tender. Approximately 20 minutes. Serves 6 to 8.

The whole world is a
Christmas tree, and stars
its many candles.

—Harriet Blodgett

# Pork & Raspberry Sauce

*Robbin Chamberlain*
*Gooseberry Patch*

*A tender roast pork that's perfect for a holiday homecoming of family!*

3 to 4-lb. rolled, boneless pork
   loin roast
1 t. salt

1 t. black pepper
1 t. sage

Preheat oven to 325 degrees. Sprinkle roast with salt, pepper and sage. Place roast on rack in shallow roasting pan. Bake for 1-1/2 to 2 hours, or until meat thermometer registers 160 degrees.

## Raspberry Sauce:

12 oz. frozen raspberries,
   thawed
3 c. sugar
1/2 c. white vinegar
1/2 t. cloves
1/2 t. ginger

1/2 t. nutmeg
1/2 c. cornstarch
2 T. lemon juice
2 T. butter, melted
6 to 8 drops red food coloring

Drain raspberries, reserving juice. Add water to juice, if necessary, to make 1-1/2 cups. Combine one cup of the raspberry liquid with sugar, vinegar, cloves, ginger and nutmeg in a saucepan. Bring to a boil. Reduce heat; simmer uncovered for 10 minutes. Blend cornstarch and remaining raspberry liquid; add to saucepan. Cook over medium heat, constantly stirring for one minute or until thickened. Stir in raspberries, lemon juice, butter and food coloring. Place roast on platter, serve with sauce. Serves 10.

# Cozy Kitchen Suppers

## Country Glazed Ham

*Juanita Williams*
*Jacksonville, OR*

*I love to serve this ham on a large platter surrounded by whole cranberries and orange slice twists.*

10 to 12-lb. fully cooked smoked    1/4 c. water
   ham, skin removed and
   fat trimmed

Preheat oven to 325 degrees. Place ham in shallow roasting pan and add water. Bake approximately 16 minutes per pound. If ham browns too quickly, place a tent of foil over it. Do not seal. When done, remove from oven and allow to rest while making the glaze.

### Glaze:

thinly sliced peels of 6 oranges    3/4 c. orange marmalade
2 c. water                          4 T. red wine
1/3 c. currant jelly

Combine orange peels and water in saucepan and boil for 10 minutes. Drain and repeat. Combine jelly, marmalade and orange peels in saucepan and simmer for 10 minutes. Remove from heat and stir in wine. Spread over ham.

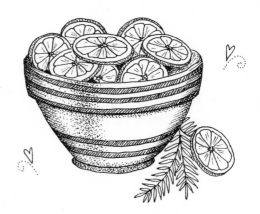

*A yellowware bowl looks wonderful filled with fresh cedar and red apples!*

# Chicken with Biscuit Topping

Jan Stafford
Chickamauga, GA

*A real comfort food!*

1/4 c. onion, chopped
1/4 c. oil
1/4 c. all-purpose flour
2-1/4 c. chicken stock
16-oz. can mixed peas
    and carrots

1/4 c. celery, sliced and cooked
2 c. chicken, cubed and cooked
salt and pepper to taste

In saucepan, sauté onion in oil until lightly browned and tender. Remove half of onion to small dish for biscuit topping. Add flour to remaining onion and oil; stir well. Blend in stock and cook, stirring constantly to thicken. Add peas, carrots, celery and chicken. Blend well. Pour mixture into 2-quart baking dish and set aside while preparing biscuits.

## Biscuit Topping:

1/3 c. shortening
reserved onions

1-1/2 c. self-rising flour
1/2 c. milk

Cut shortening and onions into flour. Add milk and stir until flour is dampened. Roll out on floured surface and cut with biscuit cutter. Carefully place biscuits on top of chicken mixture. Bake at 375 degrees for 20 minutes or until biscuits are lightly browned.

*Use fusible webbing to attach muslin cut-outs of your children's handprints to homespun pillows!*

## Classic Sauerbraten
*Jo Ann*

*Be sure to plan ahead. You need to marinate the roast two days before you plan to serve it.*

2-1/4 c. water
1 c. cider vinegar
1 med. onion, coarsely chopped
1 lemon, cut into wedges
2 bay leaves
1-1/2 t. salt
1/2 t. whole black peppercorns
1/2 t. whole cloves

4-1/2 lb. top round roast
1/4 c. vegetable oil
1/4 c. all-purpose flour
1 c. canned beef broth
1/3 c. dark brown sugar
1/3 c. gingersnap cookie crumbs
salt and pepper, to taste

Combine first 8 ingredients in large saucepan and bring to boil. Cool. Place roast in bowl slightly larger than roast. Pour marinade over. Cover and chill for 2 days, turning twice. Remove roast from marinade. Place in a Dutch oven, bake at 350 degrees until tender, approximately 2 hours. Set meat aside and cool. Pour any accumulated juices from roasting pan into marinade. Strain marinade. Do not clean roasting pan. Mix 1/4 cup oil and flour in a large skillet. Stir over medium heat for 10 minutes, or until dark brown. Gradually mix in 2 cups of marinade and broth. Boil until thick, stirring often, about 10 minutes. Mix in sugar and cookie crumbs. Pour into roasting pan and place over medium heat. Bring to a boil, scraping up any browned bits. Season to taste with salt and pepper. Slice beef and arrange in large baking dish. Pour sauce over meat. Bake at 400 degrees for 15 minutes, or until thoroughly heated through.

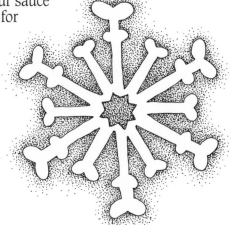

# Stuffed Beef Tenderloin

*Donna Dye*
*London, OH*

*Stuffed with spinach and cheese; this roast is so
tender you can cut it with a fork!*

10-oz. pkg. frozen chopped
   spinach, thawed and drained
2 t. balsamic vinegar
3 oz. Muenster cheese, grated
1/4 c. dried currants
1 egg

1 garlic clove, minced
1/2 t. salt
1/2 t. pepper
6-lb. beef tenderloin, butterflied
1/3 c. beef broth

Place spinach in a large mixing bowl and add vinegar, cheese,
currants, egg, garlic, salt and pepper; blend well. Open and flatten
tenderloin and spoon spinach mixture down the center of the meat.
Bring long sides of meat together, cover filling and tie with butcher's
twine at one-inch intervals. Place roast in a shallow baking dish
and and cover with beef broth. Bake uncovered for 10 minutes at
425 degrees, reduce heat to 350 degrees and bake an additional
25 minutes for rare, or 35 minutes for medium-rare. Let tenderloin
sit for 15 minutes before carving.

*Don't forget your four-legged friends! Give your puppy
a festive sweater and your cat some catnip!*

## Quick & Easy Fried Chicken

*Desi Rader*
*Delaware, OH*

*I love this recipe because it fills that craving for some good, down home, country cooking we all love...without spending hours in the kitchen. It's a terrific meal served with mashed potatoes, gravy and a crisp salad.*

3 to 4 boneless, skinless chicken
    breasts
12-oz. can evaporated milk

1 c. oil
2 c. corn flake cereal crumbs
salt and pepper, to taste

Slice chicken lengthwise to make approximately 3 strips for each breast. Place strips in a large bowl and cover with evaporated milk. Heat oil in a large skillet on high heat approximately 3 minutes until good and hot. Pour corn flake crumbs on a plate, shake excess milk off chicken strips; coat completely in crumbs, place in heated oil. Cook chicken until golden brown on both sides. Turn only once. Drain on paper towels. Salt and pepper to taste.

When you take down your tree, set it outside and redecorate with popcorn, apples and dried corn...the birds and squirrels will love it!

## Granny's Pot Roast

*Angela Harmon*
*Memphis, TN*

*My grandmother is a "young" lady at the age of 80! Her recipe*
*for pot roast is delicious and so easy.*

3 to 5-lb. pot roast
4 carrots, peeled and sliced
6 potatoes, peeled and quartered
1/4 c. oil
1/4 c. cooking wine

1/4 c. catsup
2 T. Worcestershire sauce
1 T. soy sauce
garlic salt, to taste
pepper, to taste

Place roast in a slow cooker, top with freshly cut carrots and potatoes. In medium size bowl, mix remaining ingredients together and pour over roast. Cook on low 10 to 12 hours or until tender.

Trim a wreath for your kitchen with antique
red-handled cookie cutters and mini rolling pins;
tie on a raffia bow!

# HoMeMaDe DesSeRTs

## Grandma's Blackberry Cobbler

*Shellie Prater*
*Lubbock, TX*

*When I was very young, my grandparents lived on a ranch in northern California. Every August the whole family would gather to pick blackberries that grew at the back of the pasture. We would collect buckets and buckets of the berries; very often eating more berries than we put in our bucket! At the end of the day we stumbled back to the house stained from head to toe with blackberry juice.*

| | |
|---|---|
| 8 to 10 c. blackberries | 2-1/3 c. biscuit baking mix |
| 3/4 c. plus 3 T. sugar | 2/3 c. milk |
| 2 T. corn starch | |
| 2 T. plus 3 T. butter, divided and melted | |

Place berries in a saucepan over medium-high heat, stir occasionally until berries begin to turn liquid. Mix 3/4 cup sugar and corn starch; combine with berries and stir until mixture comes to a boil. Add additional sugar to taste. Stir 2 tablespoons melted butter into berry mixture and pour into 13"x9" pan. Combine remaining 3 tablespoons butter, biscuit baking mix, milk and 3 tablespoons sugar. Drop biscuit mixture onto berries by the spoonful. Bake at 450 degrees for 20 to 30 minutes or until golden brown. Makes 4 to 6 servings.

Thread old-fashioned chandelier crystals with wire and tie a ribbon around the top of each...beautiful ornaments for your Christmas tree.

## Lebkuchen

*Nancy Hascall*
*Otsego, MI*

*This was Grandma's favorite recipe. When I was little, we'd bake these cookies together, her arms around me and her hand on mine, helping me stir the heavy batter.*

1-1/2 c. sugar
1-1/2 c. honey
4 eggs, beaten
1/8 t. salt
2 t. cinnamon
1 t. cloves
1/2 t. allspice

1 t. baking soda
1/2 c. almonds, ground
1 c. walnuts, ground
1 c. citron, finely chopped
5 c. all-purpose flour
almond slices
1 egg yolk

Mix sugar, honey, eggs and salt thoroughly with blender. Blend in remaining ingredients, except almond slices and egg yolk. Mix well and refrigerate overnight. On a baking sheet, flatten teaspoons of batter with the bottom of a floured glass. Place an almond slice in the center of each cookie and bake at 350 degrees for 12 minutes. Remove from oven and immediately brush tops of hot cookies with egg yolk. Makes 7 dozen.

A small kitchen tree is perfect for displaying your collection of spoons or cookie cutters. Tie them on with homespun bows.

# Sugar Cream Pie

*Esther Robinson*
*Brownsville, TX*

*Your family will love it! You'll need to make more than one pie
though; they disappear quickly!*

3/4 c. sugar
1/4 c. corn starch
1 pt. half-and-half
1/2 stick plus 1 T. butter, melted

1 t. vanilla extract
9-inch pie crust, prebaked
cinnamon

Mix sugar and corn starch thoroughly in saucepan. Add half-and-half
and 1/2 stick of butter; cook until mixture boils and becomes thick;
stir constantly. Remove from heat and stir in vanilla. Let cool for a few
minutes and pour into pie crust. Drizzle one tablespoon butter over top
and sprinkle with cinnamon. Place under broiler one to 2 minutes or
until pie mixture bubbles. Cool and serve.

Holiday guests will feel
extra-special if you dress
their bed in cozy red and
green flannel sheets;
add a cozy quilt, too!

# ♥ HoMeMaDe DesSeRTS ♥

## Candy Cane Thumbprints

*Jennifer Martineau*
*Delaware, OH*

*My little daughter insists on making the thumbprints herself...
won't Santa love finding a plate of these cookies on Christmas Eve!*

| | |
|---|---|
| 2/3 c. butter, softened | 1 egg, beaten |
| 1/2 c. sugar | 1 t. vanilla extract |
| 1/4 t. salt | 1-1/2 c. all-purpose flour |

With an electric mixer on low speed, blend butter, sugar and salt. Mix
in egg and vanilla. Beat in as much flour as possible; stir in remaining
flour. Cover; chill for one hour. Shape dough into one-inch balls; place
2 inches apart on ungreased baking sheets. Bake at 375 degrees for
8 to 10 minutes, until lightly golden around edges. Remove from oven;
make a thumbprint in each cookie with thumb. Cool. Pipe filling into
centers; sprinkle with crushed candy. Makes about 3 dozen.

## Filling:

| | |
|---|---|
| 1/4 c. butter, softened | 1-1/2 c. powdered sugar |
| 1/4 t. peppermint extract | 2 to 3 t. milk |

Blend butter and extract. Gradually add powdered sugar and milk to a
piping consistency.

*Fill a hurricane globe with nuts, fruit and
small ornaments for a lovely centerpiece!*

# Ginger Creams

*Marilyn Wright*
*Hilton, NY*

*This recipe has been handed down in our family...from my grandmother, mother and now, me. We've always made these for Christmas.*

1/4 c. shortening
1/2 c. sugar
1 egg, beaten
1/2 c. molasses
2 c. all-purpose flour
1/2 t. salt

1 t. ginger
1/2 t. nutmeg
1/2 t. cloves
1/2 t. cinnamon
1 t. baking soda
1/2 c. hot water

In a bowl, cream together shortening and sugar, blend in egg and molasses. In a separate bowl, combine flour and salt with spices, sifting well. Thoroughly blend into egg mixture. Dissolve baking soda in water, stirring well; blend into dough. Drop by teaspoonfuls on an ungreased baking sheet and bake at 400 degrees for 8 minutes. Cool completely and frost with your favorite powdered sugar icing.

Cover the lids of homemade preserve jars with brown paper and secure with a ribbon. Glue a row of buttons to the ribbon ends.

## Maple Meltaways

*Jo Ann*

*This delicious cookie is perfect for mailing in holiday care packages.*

2 c. all-purpose flour
1 c. butter, softened
3/4 c. sugar

1-1/2 t. maple extract
1/4 t. salt
2/3 c. pecan halves

Combine first 5 ingredients together in a large bowl; beat until fluffy.
Drop dough by rounded teaspoonfuls onto an ungreased cookie sheet.
Press a pecan half in the center of each cookie. Bake at 350 degrees for
10 minutes or until lightly brown.  Remove to a wire rack to cool.
Makes 4 dozen cookies.

## Sugared Apples

*Mary Lou Traylor*
*Arlington, TN*

*A sweet treat on Christmas Eve!*

1/4 c. flour
1/2 t. cinnamon
1/4 t. nutmeg
1/8 t. salt

1/4 c. vegetable oil
4 lg. Granny Smith apples,
   seeded and sliced
powdered sugar

Mix flour, cinnamon, nutmeg and salt together in a shallow dish.
Heat oil in heavy skillet until hot. Coat apple slices in flour mixture
and fry 6 to 8 minutes. Set on paper towels and dust with powdered
sugar. Serve warm.

# Ginger Cookies

*Tina Stidam*
*Delaware, OH*

*We leave these cookies for Santa each year!*

| | |
|---|---|
| 2/3 c. vegetable oil | 2 t. baking soda |
| 1 c. plus 1/2 c. sugar, divided | 1 t. cinnamon |
| 4 T. light molasses | 1 t. ginger |
| 1 egg, beaten | 1/2 t. salt |
| 2 c. all-purpose flour | |

In large bowl, combine oil, one cup sugar and remaining ingredients together. Mix well and roll dough into balls. Place remaining sugar in a small bowl and roll each ball in the sugar. Place 1-1/2 to 2 inches apart on an ungreased cookie sheet and bake at 350 degrees for 9 to 11 minutes. Makes approximately 6 dozen cookies.

Invite friends and neighbors over for an old-fashioned tree-trimming party! Pull out all your favorite ornaments, have holiday music playing and serve lots of yummy snacks!

## Apple Crumble Pie

*Michelle McKenney*
*Hamburg, NJ*

*A wonderful, homemade apple pie. Enjoy a slice topped with a scoop of cinnamon ice cream.*

9-inch pie crust, unbaked
3 T. all-purpose flour
1/8 t. allspice
1/4 t. nutmeg
1/4 t. ginger
1 t. cinnamon

4 T. butter, divided and cut
   into pieces
5 c. apples, peeled and
   thinly sliced
1/2 c. sugar
1/2 c. dark brown sugar

Unwrap pie crust and place into an 8-1/2" pie plate. Set aside. In a small bowl, mix together flour and spices. Add 2 tablespoons butter to the flour mixture, mixing well with a pastry blender; set aside. In a large bowl, mix together apples and sugars; stir in flour mixture. Add to the pie crust and top with remaining 2 tablespoons butter.

### Crumble Topping:

1 c. all-purpose flour
1 c. dark brown sugar
1 stick butter, softened
1 t. cinnamon
1/4 t. ginger
1/4 t. nutmeg
1/8 t. allspice
Garnish: cinnamon

Mix all ingredients together. Place topping over apple pie mixture. Sprinkle with as much cinnamon as desired. Bake at 375 degrees for 30 minutes. Remove pie from the oven and cover the pie crust with foil or a pie crust shield. Return to the oven and continue baking for another 30 minutes.

# Hard Tac Candy Treats

*Christi Miller*
*New Paris, PA*

*When I was a little girl, my mom and I would spend an evening together at Chrismastime making this candy.*

1 c. water
1/2 c. light corn syrup
2 c. sugar

1/2 t. flavored oils used for candy making
food coloring

Combine first 3 ingredients in a heavy pan. Using a candy thermometer, continue to cook until mixture reaches 310 degrees. Remove from heat and add flavoring and as much food coloring as desired. Pour onto a greased jelly roll pan. When cool enough to handle, cut or break into squares.

# Apple Raisin Cobbler Pie

*Vickie*

*A sweet, warm treat when there's a chill in the air!*

2 20-oz. cans apple pie filling
1 c. raisins
1/4 t. nutmeg
9-inch shortbread ready-made pie crust

1/3 c. all-purpose flour
1/4 c. brown sugar, packed
3 T. butter, melted
3/4 c. walnuts, chopped

In a small bowl, combine pie filling, raisins and nutmeg; spoon into crust. In a separate bowl, combine flour and brown sugar; cut in butter until crumbly. Stir in walnuts and sprinkle over filling. Bake at 375 degrees for 35 to 45 minutes until golden.

## German Chocolate Cake

*Sharon Pruess*
*South Ogden, UT*

*No visit to my grandparents' farm would be complete without a fresh glass of milk and a big slice of my Grandma's German chocolate cake!*

1 pkg. white cake mix
5.9-oz. pkg. instant chocolate
  pudding
1 c. milk
1 c. water
3 egg whites

Combine all ingredients in a large bowl and beat at medium speed for 2 minutes. Pour into 2 greased and floured round cake pans. Bake at 350 degrees for 25 to 35 minutes. Cool 10 minutes in pans and remove. Cool completely before frosting.

### Frosting:

1 c. evaporated milk
1 c. sugar
3 egg yolks, slightly beaten
1/2 c. butter, melted
1 t. vanilla extract
1-1/3 c. shredded coconut
1 c. pecans, chopped

Combine evaporated milk, sugar, egg yolks, butter and vanilla in a saucepan. Cook over medium heat, stirring constantly for approximately 12 minutes, or until thick. Remove from heat and add coconut and pecans. Beat until mixture is cool and spreadable; frost cake.

*Tie shiny red or green apples with strips of homespun and pile in a wooden bowl.*

# Lemon Chess Pie

*Ricki Treleaven*
*Birmingham, AL*

*An old-fashioned favorite we love!*

| | |
|---|---|
| 1/2 c. butter | 1 t. lemon extract |
| 1-1/3 c. sugar | 1 T. white vinegar |
| 3 jumbo eggs | 1/3 c. milk |
| 2 T. cornmeal | 9" pie crust, unbaked |

Cream butter and sugar together. Stir in eggs and cornmeal. Blend in lemon extract, vinegar and milk, pour into pie crust. Bake at 350 degrees for 45 to 60 minutes, or until center is set.

Paint a bushel basket inside and out. When dry, hand-letter or stencil your children's names on the front. Fill their personalized basket with gifts!

## Peanut Butter Fudge

*Ruth Naples*
*Mexico, ME*

*This recipe was shared with me by a pen-pal. It's very easy to make and perfect if you're looking for candy to tuck in a package and mail during the holidays.*

1 lb. sugar
1 lb. light brown sugar
3/4 c. milk
18 oz. peanut butter

7-1/2 oz. jar marshmallow
   creme
1 c. peanuts, chopped
1 t. vanilla extract

Mix sugar, brown sugar and milk in a large saucepan. Bring slowly to a boil, stirring constantly so as not to burn. Allow to boil for 5 minutes. Remove from heat and add peanut butter, marshmallow creme, nuts and vanilla; mix quickly before fudge hardens. Pour mixture into 2 well-buttered 8"x8" pans. Allow to set until firm. Cut into squares.

Add a special decoration to your favorite gingerbread recipe. When it's cooled, place a large stencil on top and dust with powdered sugar, gently remove the stencil! You can use tiny stencils, too. Cut the gingerbread into squares, put a tiny stencil on each one, sprinkle with sugar.

# Apple Crunch

*Wendy Lee Paffenroth*
*Pine Island, NY*

*Our family likes to top this with crunchy cinnamon cereal
for a special treat!*

4 c. apples, thinly sliced
1/3 c. all-purpose flour
1 c. oatmeal
1/2 c. sugar
1/2 c. brown sugar
1 t. vanilla extract

1 t. almond extract
1/3 c. butter, cut into pieces
1 t. cinnamon
1-1/2 c. corn flake cereal
Garnish: cinnamon

Arrange one layer of apples in an oiled pie pan. Mix remaining apples
with flour, oatmeal, sugars, extracts, butter and cinnamon. Spoon
mixture on top of apples. Top with cereal and sprinkle with cinnamon.
Bake at 350 degrees for approximately 30 minutes or until apples are
soft and the pie is bubbly.

Create a cookie wreath for your family! On a
circular serving tray, place leaf-shaped cookies with
green icing. Layer colorful star, snowflake or
heart-shaped cookies on top.

# ♥ HoMeMaDe DesSeRTS ♥

## Old-Fashioned Cream Pie

*Laura Cottrell*
*Payne, OH*

*My Aunt Faye is famous for this recipe...she isn't allowed to come to a family gathering without it! I remember as a child, we had to cut the pie into very small slivers so everyone could have a piece!*

1/3 c. all-purpose flour
1/3 c. sugar
2/3 c. brown sugar, packed
1/2 pt. whipping cream

1 c. half-and-half
8-inch pie crust, unbaked
Garnish: cinnamon

Mix flour, sugar and brown sugar together; blend well. Add whipping cream and mix well. Scald half-and-half; do not boil. Add to the whipping cream mixture and stir well. Pour into pie crust and sprinkle with as much cinnamon as desired. Bake 15 minutes at 375 degrees, then reduce heat to 350 degrees and bake an additional 30 to 35 minutes. When pie is lightly browned and bubbly, remove from oven and place on rack to cool. Let cool completely before cutting.

Dab water-soluble paint over decorative paper doilies on each windowpane...the snowflake designs easily wipe off with a damp sponge! You can also add wintry snowflakes to mirrors and car windows, too.

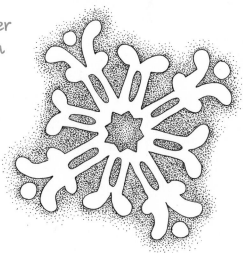

# Cinnamon Pudding Cake

*Phyllis Peters*
*Three Rivers, MI*

*A terrific dessert for a chilly winter evening! Serve with
a mug of homemade cocoa!*

1 c. sugar
2 T. butter
1 c. milk
2 c. all-purpose flour

2 t. baking powder
2 t. cinnamon
1/4 t. salt

Mix all ingredients together and
blend well. Pour into a greased
13"x9" baking pan, add topping.

## Topping:

2 c. brown sugar
2 T. butter
1-1/4 c. water

Combine ingredients in a saucepan; bring to a boil. Pour mixture over
the cake batter and bake at 350 degrees for 25 minutes. Serves 12.

You can turn the container you tuck your
cookies and candy into, part of the gift! Antique
fluted pudding molds, old-fashioned tea cups and
tea pots, hatboxes or vintage cookie jars are just
right for gift-giving. Add your treat inside
then wrap with holiday ribbon or lengths
of dimestore rickrack.

## Mary's Christmas Cookies

Susan Bowman
Moline, IL

*My high school friend, Mary, and I are fortunate to still live in the same area. We enjoyed these cookies at Mary's house many years ago and they are still one of my favorites! They're easy, yummy and perfect for a Christmas cookie exchange!*

1 c. butter
1 c. brown sugar
1 egg
1 t. vanilla extract

2 c. all-purpose flour
8  1.55 oz. chocolate bars
1/2 to 1 c. nuts, chopped

Cream butter and brown sugar together. Add egg, vanilla and flour. Spread into a 15"x10" jelly roll pan. Bake at 350 degrees for 15 to 20 minutes. Remove from oven and add chocolate bars while still hot. Let chocolate bars melt and spread over top. Sprinkle with chopped nuts and cut into small squares.

*Cross a pair of snowshoes and wire to the front of an evergreen wreath!*

# Orange Mallow Pie

*Deberah Green*
*Gooseberry Patch*

*This is an easy holiday dessert and the orange taste is so refreshing.*

3 c. miniature marshmallows
1 T. orange zest, grated
3/4 c. orange juice

2 T. lemon juice
1-1/2 c. whipping cream, chilled
9-inch pie crust, prebaked

Cook marshmallows, orange zest and juices over low heat until marshmallows melt. Stir in whipping cream; blend well and spread into pie crust. Refrigerate for 4 hours.

# Cream Cheese Pound Cake

*Mary Lou Traylor*
*Arlington, TN*

*We like to serve this sliced and toasted. We top it with a combination of cherry pie filling and cream cheese, then sprinkle with a dash of cinnamon.*

3/4 lb. butter
8-oz. pkg. cream cheese
3 c. sugar
6 eggs

1 t. vanilla extract
1 t. almond extract
3 c. all-purpose flour

Cream together butter and cream cheese, blend in sugar. Add eggs, one at a time, and beat until smooth. Add extracts and flour, mix until smooth. Pour into greased and floured 10" tube pan. Bake at 325 degrees for 1-1/2 to 2 hours until cake is golden and toothpick inserted comes out clean.

# ❤ Homemade Desserts ❤

## Hot Milk Sponge Cake

*Cheryl Volbruck*
*Costa Mesa, CA*

*In our family of seven, my mother always had something good cooking and the wonderful aroma filled our house. This was one of the first recipes I asked her for. It's a unique recipe because it doesn't have any shortening in the ingredients. The recipe was handed down from Mom's great grandmother and we would beg for it on our birthdays! To honor Mom, and all that she's done for us over the years, I'm sharing our favorite recipe.*

4 eggs, lightly beaten
2 c. sugar
1 c. milk, scalded then cooled
1 t. vanilla extract

2-1/2 c. all-purpose flour
2 t. baking powder
1/4 t. salt

Combine eggs and sugar, mixing well. Blend in milk and vanilla. Add the remaining dry ingredients and stir with a wooden spoon. Pour into an ungreased Bundt® or tube pan. Bake at 300 degrees for 40 to 60 minutes, or until a toothpick inserted in the center comes out clean. To cool, place pan upside down over a funnel or large bottle. While still warm, loosen edges and remove cake from pan.

Antique thread spools can be made into old-fashioned candleholders...tuck in a small taper, add holly berries, sprigs of greenery and a bow.

# Caramel Apple Crisp

Pat Habiger
Spearville, KS

*Our family loves to enjoy this recipe when the weather turns chilly!*

| | |
|---|---|
| 1/2 c. all-purpose flour | 40 caramels, quartered |
| 1/2 c. sugar | 9 c. baking apples, peeled |
| 1/2 t. cinnamon | and sliced |
| 1/4 t. nutmeg | 1/4 c. orange juice |

Combine flour, sugar, cinnamon and nutmeg; add caramels and stir to coat. In a separate bowl, toss apples with orange juice. Stir in caramel mixture and spread into a greased 13"x9" baking pan. Add topping.

## Topping:

| | |
|---|---|
| 1/2 c. sugar | 2/3 c. quick-cooking oats |
| 1/3 c. all-purpose flour | 1/2 c. walnuts, chopped |
| 3 T. butter | |

Combine sugar and flour in a small bowl; cut in butter until crumbly. Add oats and walnuts; sprinkle over apples. Bake at 350 degrees for 30 to 40 minutes, or until apples are tender. Makes 16 to 20 servings.

Small cheer and
great welcome makes
a merry feast.

—William Shakespeare

# ♥ HoMeMaDe DeSSeRTS ♥

## Old-Fashioned Spicy Pumpkin Pie

*Roberta Clark*
*Delaware, OH*

*This is a favorite recipe! Our family enjoys it as a special treat to top off any meal...especially a holiday dinner!*

4 eggs, beaten
2 c. brown sugar
1/4 t. nutmeg
1 t. ginger
3 t. cinnamon
1/2 t. mace

1/2 t. cloves
1 t. salt
2 T. molasses
3 c. pumpkin
2 c. evaporated milk
2 9-inch pie crusts, prebaked

Blend eggs, brown sugar, spices, salt, molasses and pumpkin. Thoroughly blend and add evaporated milk. Mix well and pour into crusts. Bake in a preheated oven at 450 degrees for 10 minutes, then reduce heat to 350 degrees for 30 minutes or until center of pie is set.

Fill an old sap bucket with pine cones and twiggy rosehip branches.

## Great Grandma's Christmas Cookies
*Stacey Weichert*
*Moorhead, MN*

*This recipe has been in my family for over 100 years. My earliest memory is of baking these cookies with my family. For aprons, my Grandma pinned white flour sack dish towels around my two older sisters and myself. We stood on chairs pushed up to the counter on both sides of Great-Grandma Sunny. She would cut the cookies out with a round biscuit cutter and our job was to cut out a little circle from the center of each cookie with a silver thimble. My mom would be busy frosting the cookies and we all helped with sprinkles. The cookies were then carefully packed into tins and placed in the freezer until the week of Christmas.*

2 c. brown sugar
1 c. shortening
1 egg, beaten
1/2 c. buttermilk
4 c. all-purpose flour, divided

4 T. cocoa
1 t. cinnamon
1/8 t. salt
1 t. baking soda

Cream brown sugar with shortening. Mix in egg and buttermilk. In separate bowl, blend together 2 cups flour, cocoa, cinnamon, salt and baking soda. Add flour mixture to the brown sugar mixture; add enough of the remaining flour to make a stiff dough. Roll out and cut with a biscuit cutter. Cut a thimble-size center hole in the middle. Bake at 350 degrees for 12 to 14 minutes. When cool, frost with your favorite powdered sugar frosting.

*A blue spatterware bucket looks great filled with bright red apples.*

# ♥ Homemade Desserts ♥

## Molasses Gingersnap Cookies

*Kristine Gilbert*
*Bath, NY*

*My very favorite cookie is my Grandma Crane's. I remember these cookies being a staple at her home and I couldn't wait until Grandma let me help her make these. I remember her patience with me at my first attempts. One of the secrets she let me in on was to never make the dough balls the size suggested...they just weren't big enough, we had to make cookies of substance!*

2 to 2-1/2 c. sugar, divided
1-1/2 c. shortening
2 eggs
1/2 c. molasses
4 c. all-purpose flour

2 t. cinnamon
2 t. cloves
2 t. ginger
2 t. baking soda
Optional: 1 c. raisins

Cream 2 cups sugar and shortening; add the eggs and beat until smooth. Stir in molasses, blending well. Sift dry ingredients together and add one cup at a time to the shortening mixture. Mix in raisins, if desired. The dough will be very stiff, so make sure that it is well-blended. Roll into one-inch balls, and roll in additional 1/2 cup sugar. Place 2 inches apart on an ungreased cookie sheet and bake at 375 degrees for 12 to 13 minutes. Makes approximately 5 dozen.

*Add a light dusting of sugar or edible glitter to the tops of your cookies to create a delightful frosted effect!*

# Fondant

*Marjorie Foland*
*Wilmington, OH*

*While I was growing up, our family would begin making candy on the first Sunday afternoon in December and continue each Sunday until Christmas. It was such a wonderful "together" time. Dad always cracked the nuts and my two brothers licked the pans!*

2 c. sugar
1 c. milk
2 T. margarine

1 t. vanilla extract
Garnish: pecan halves

Combine sugar and milk in a saucepan and cook to a soft ball stage; 238 degrees on a candy thermometer. Remove from heat. Add margarine and vanilla; cool. Using a heavy-duty mixer, or kneading by hand, mix until stiff enough to shape into balls. Using approximately one teaspoonful, roll fondant into balls and top each ball with 1/2 of a pecan. Makes approximately 40 pieces of fondant.

*Tie a festive ribbon around an old sugar bucket. Line the inside with plastic and partially fill with pebbles. Tuck in paperwhite bulbs and water to cover the pebbles...in no time you'll have blooming flowers in winter!*

# ♥ Homemade Desserts ♥

## Chocolate Layer Pie

*Becky Sykes*
*Gooseberry Patch*

*A chocolate-lovers dream!*

1 c. all-purpose flour
1 stick butter, melted
1 c. plus 2 t. powdered sugar, divided
1 c. pecans, chopped
8-oz. pkg. cream cheese, softened

12-oz. pkg. frozen whipped topping, thawed
3 c. milk
2 3.5-oz. pkg. instant chocolate pudding

Mix flour, butter, 2 teaspoons of powdered sugar and pecans. Pat into a 13"x9" pan. Bake at 350 degrees for 10 to 20 minutes and cool. Mix cream cheese, one cup powdered sugar and half of the whipped topping; spread on cooled crust. Blend milk and pudding; stirring until thick; spread over cream cheese layer. Spread remainder of whipped topping on top and refrigerate until ready to serve.

Kids will enjoy Christmas snow cones! Gather a pail of freshly-fallen snow and top with their favorite flavor fruit juice. Make an old-fashioned treat by drizzling warm maple syrup over a a bowl of fresh snow!

# Sugar Plums

*Delores Berg*
*Selah, WA*

*These are a Christmas tradition at our house...they are yummy!*

2 eggs, beaten
1-1/2 c. sugar, divided
1 c. dates, chopped

1 c. coconut
1 c. walnuts, chopped
1 t. vanilla extract

Blend eggs and one cup sugar together. Stir in dates, coconut, walnuts and vanilla. Butter a 2-quart casserole dish and pour in mixture. Bake at 375 degrees for 30 minutes, stirring every 10 minutes. Remove from oven and let cool until mixture can be handled, Roll into walnut-size balls. Roll balls in remaining sugar.

*Make a cookie cutter wreath! Arrange cutters in a circle, with edges touching, and glue each in place with a glue gun.*

## Praline Banana Cake

*Eileen Steitz-Watts*
*East Brunswick, NJ*

*My childhood memories of visits to Grandma Doyle's were always a delightful experience. Grandma was devoted to her family and her meals were a delight! She began sharing her recipes with me when I was only 8 or 9 years old because even back then, I wanted to cook and bake like she did.*

1 c. light brown sugar, firmly
   packed
3/4 stick unsalted butter,
   softened
3/4 c. pecan halves
2 lg. ripe bananas, peeled
   and sliced
1-1/2 c. cake flour

1 c. ripe bananas, peeled
   and mashed
1/2 c. buttermilk
1 t. vanilla extract
1-1/4 c. sugar
1/3 c. shortening
2 eggs

Cream brown sugar and butter in medium bowl until well mixed. Spread in a 9"x9" glass baking dish. Arrange pecan halves over brown sugar mixture, layer banana slices over pecans, covering completely. Measure cake flour in a bowl; set aside. In a separate bowl, combine mashed bananas, buttermilk and vanilla. Using an electric mixer, cream sugar and shortening until fluffy. Add eggs one at a time, beating well after each addition. Alternate adding dry ingredients with buttermilk mixture until well-blended. Pour over bananas. Bake at 350 degrees for approximately one hour and 5 minutes or until toothpick comes out clean. Cool and invert cake on plate. Serve warm.

# Christmas Butter Fudge

*Juanita Williams*
*Jacksonville, OR*

*An old-fashioned recipe that's perfect to share with your neighbors.*
*Tuck your fudge into stenciled Shaker boxes or decorated tins.*

4 c. sugar
2 c. milk
1 stick butter
1/4 t. salt

1 t. vanilla extract
1/4 c. candied cherries, finely
   chopped
1/4 c. pistachios, blanched

Combine sugar, milk, butter and salt in large saucepan. Bring to a boil, stirring constantly until sugar is dissolved. Cook over medium heat, stirring occasionally, until candy thermometer reads 236 degrees. Remove from heat immediately; set pan in cold water. Do not stir or beat until cooled to lukewarm. Add vanilla; beat until candy becomes thick, creamy and loses its shine. When at setting point, add cherries and nuts; fold in quickly. Pour into buttered 8" square pan. Let stand at room temperature until firm. Cut into squares; decorate with candied fruit on top. Makes 2-1/2 pounds.

With pomp, power and glory the world beckons vainly, in chase of such vanities why should I roam? While peace and content bless my little thatched cottage, and warm my own hearth with the treasures of home.

—Beatrix Potter

# ❤ ℌOMEMADE DESSERTS ❤

## Apple Dumpling Roll

*Margaret Scoresby*
*Mount Vernon, OH*

*You can serve this wonderful apple treat warm or cold!*

3-1/2 c. tart apples, thinly sliced
4 T. plus 3/4 c. sugar, divided
1/2 c. water
2 T. lemon juice
1 T. butter
1-1/4 c. all-purpose flour
3 t. baking powder

1/4 t. salt
1/4 c. shortening
1 egg, beaten
1/2 c. milk
1/2 c. brown sugar
cinnamon

Preheat oven to 375 degrees. Combine apples, 2 tablespoons sugar and water. Boil for 5 minutes. Drain apples; reserve syrup. Measure 3/4 cup syrup. Adding water if necessary; pour syrup into 8"x8" baking pan. Stir in 3/4 cup sugar, lemon juice and butter. Place baking pan in preheated oven while preparing rolls. In a large bowl, sift flour, 2 tablespoons sugar, baking powder and salt. Cut in shortening to resemble coarse meal. In a separate bowl, combine egg and milk. Add to flour mixture; stir with a fork. Transfer dough to floured board, and pat into 18"x12" rectangle. Cover dough with drained apples. Sprinkle with brown sugar and cinnamon. Roll, jelly-roll style and cut into 2-inch slices. Place slices, cut side down, in syrup in 8"x8" pan. Bake 30 minutes or until lightly browned. Serve with lemon sauce.

## Lemon Sauce:

1/2 c. sugar
2 T. cornstarch
1/4 t. salt
1 c. water

1 lemon rind, grated
1/4 c. lemon juice
2 T. butter

Mix first 3 ingredients in small saucepan. Add 1/4 cup of water and blend. Add remaining water and bring to a boil; stirring constantly. Boil until thickened and clear. Remove from heat and add remaining ingredients.

# Gingerbread Men

*Phyllis Peters*
*Three Rivers, MI*

*Each year as I open the book and read delightful words to very
interested listeners, I share the story of the gingerbread boy with the
next generation. Here is our recipe for you to try; start a tradition in
your own family.*

1 c. butter
1 c. sugar
2 eggs, beaten
1/2 c. molasses

4-1/2 c. all-purpose flour
2 t. ginger
1 t. baking soda
1/2 t. salt, optional

Cream butter and sugar, add the remaining ingredients and blend well;
dough will be stiff. Roll out to 1/4-inch thickness, cut out gingerbread
men with a cookie cutter. Place on a lightly greased cookie sheet and
bake at 400 degrees for 10 to 12 minutes. Remove from oven and
cool. Decorate as desired. Makes about 20 cookies.

*A wooden bowl filled with pomegranates, lady apples and
juniper makes a welcoming country centerpiece.*

# Sponge-Painted Christmas Tins

*Terri Vanden Bosch*
*Rock Valley, IA*

*This is quick and easy, and can hold a variety of holiday gifts...*
*cookies, mixes, candy or jars of homemade jam. I also use*
*them as napkin and silverware holders.*

tin can, any size, lid removed
spray paint
1-inch square kitchen sponges
assorted acrylic paints

permanent black marker
electric drill with a small bit
16 gauge black wire

Spray paint the outside and bottom of your container; let the paint cure
for several days. Use sponges to sponge paint a border of color on the
top and bottom edges of can. In the space in between, any design can
be added...primitive hearts, snowmen and trees look nice, and can be
painted on with sponge to give it a look of hand-painted pottery.
When the paint is dry add the details and outline your pictures with
the black marker. Drill holes on opposite sides of the container. Cut a
12-inch length of wire and wrap around a pencil to curl the wire and
add texture. Thread through the holes and twist
the ends tightly to form the handle.

You can stencil a
pattern on your
tin, too! Lay the
stencil on and
secure with tape.
Dip your sponge
into paint, blot
off excess and
gently press into
stencil openings.

# ❧ Holiday Trimmings ❧

## Stenciled Tissue Paper

*Joanne West*
*Beavercreek, OH*

*Two fun ways of creating personalized wrapping.*

tissue paper                          stenciling brush
stencil                                acrylic paints

Lay tissue paper flat, place stencil along one edge. Dip your brush in
paint and slowly speckle paint through the stencil opening. Carefully
lift up stencil being sure not to crease tissue. Lay stencil back down on
tissue making sure to line stencil up with the last pattern created.
Repeat until tissue paper is covered and let dry. Drying time will
depend on the type of paint used, usually a couple of hours to a couple
of days. Leave flat while drying.

## Stenciled Gift Wrap

brown kraft paper                     stenciling brush
stencil                                acrylic paint

To give texture to the surface, scrunch kraft paper into a ball, being
sure to press firmly to crease. Flatten the paper out and iron on low
heat from the middle of the paper to the outside edges. Place stencil
in the upper left corner of the paper. After stencil is placed, begin to
speckle paint through the stencil. Lift stencil and place next to
completed pattern, being sure to line up. Repeat this process until
paper is covered. Let dry thoroughly.

# Grocery Bag Wrapping Paper

*Sue Carter Moore*
*Marcy, OH*

*Remember not to use brown kraft paper for this gift wrap; it won't absorb the water as quickly or give you the same finished texture, which is part of this paper's charm!*

brown paper grocery bag  
scissors  
natural sponge  

assorted craft paints  
paper plate  

Cut from the top of the bag along the seam line toward the bottom of the bag. Cut around the bottom of the bag in the fold line to remove bottom. Cut seam line away so that what remains is a rectangle of paper. Take the brown bag rectangle and run warm water over it, crushing it into a ball, and wringing out excess water. For one minute, wring very dry while continuing to keep the ball shape in order to add wrinkles. Flatten the wet bag on a counter top, printed side down. Smooth the edges and keep the paper reasonably flat. Select colors for sponging and place 2, 3 or 4 different colors of paint, about a quarter in size, on a paper plate. Wet the sponge; wring excess water out. Dab several colors of paint on the sponge, being careful not to overlap colors and dab over the bag at random until you achieve a pattern that you like. Hang the paper to dry as you would a towel, but don't fold in half over a clothes line or a hard crease will develop. Hanging by the edge will create a flat piece of paper that can be used in a variety of ways. This will only take about 10 minutes to do, and the paper will dry quickly. The edges and bottom of the paper bag can be used for matching or contrasting tags.

# ❧ Holiday Trimmings ❧

## Gift-Filled Jar Candle

*Boni Schultz*
*Maquoketa, IA*

*This makes a quick and creative gift!*

glass canning jar
votive holder

votive candle
length of homespun or raffia

Wash and thoroughly dry canning jar. Inside jar, place any small gifts that fit inside. For your children's teacher you might tuck in a box of chalk, 6-inch ruler, eraser, pencils, stickers or a small wooden apple. For a gardening friend, spring-blooming bulbs, vegetable seed packets, or flower seeds from your own garden would be a welcome gift. If you know someone who likes to sew or quilt, add a variety of colorful spools of thread, a thimble, old-fashioned buttons and embroidery floss. After you have filled the jar, place the votive holder inside the lip of the jar, drop the votive inside so lip of jar securely holds votive holder. Tie on a homespun or raffia bow, being sure bow does not touch candle.

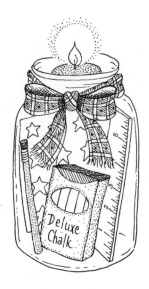

Sponge paint the outside of your jar if you
want to "hide" the gift inside!

# Handmade Gift Tags

*Dorothy Foor*
*Jeromesville, OH*

*The kids will love coloring these gift tags. Start with these easy designs, then create your own patterns!*

colored pencils
permanent, fine-point marker
colored construction paper
glue stick

hole punch
raffia
ribbon

Photocopy gift tags, enlarging size as needed. Use pencils to color gift tags; cut out. Use marker to write greeting on tag. Trace gift tag design onto construction paper, leaving a 1/8-inch border around design. Cut out and glue colored tag on top of construction paper pattern, smoothing out any wrinkles. Punch hole in the corner of the gift tag and attach to gift with raffia or ribbon.

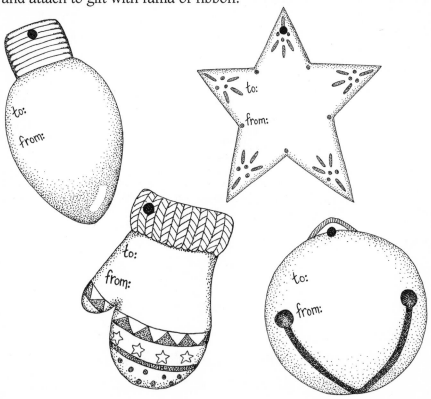

## Edible Cookie Bowl

*Eleanor Bierley*
*Miamisburg, OH*

*You can freeze your cookie bowl for up to a month,
thaw it out and then tuck in fresh holiday cut-outs!*

1-1/4 c. all-purpose flour
1/2 c. unsweetened cocoa
  powder
1/4 c. almonds, blanched and
  finely ground
1/2 t. salt
1/2 stick margarine, softened
2/3 c. sugar

1 egg
1/2 t. vanilla extract
assorted cookies
round oven-proof bowl
1-1/2 inch cookie cutter with
  scalloped edges

In a medium bowl, mix together flour, cocoa powder, almonds and salt. In a large bowl, beat together margarine, sugar, egg and vanilla. Blend in flour mixture. Roll dough to 1/8-inch thickness, cut out shapes. Cover the outside of the round oven-proof bowl with foil and spray with cooking spray. On the outside of round bowl, gently place cut-outs, slightly overlapping them. Bake the cookie bowl at 350 degrees for 10 to 12 minutes or until cookie bowl is firm. Transfer to a wire rack and cool. Carefully lift the cookie bowl off the round bowl;remove foil.

While your neighbors are away, surprise them
by building a jolly snowman in their yard!

# Balsam Draft Stoppers

*Liz Plotnick-Snay*
*Gooseberry Patch*

*Give your homemade potpourri in this homespun draft stopper!*

36"x12" homespun fabric
3/4" wide fusible web, 36" long
balsam or evergreen scented
   potpourri
2 rubber bands

6 yds. natural raffia
sprigs of pine
small pine cones
glue gun

Remove horizontal threads from each short end of fabric to make a 1/2-inch fringe. Lay fabric flat, printed side up, and fuse a strip of webbing to one 36-inch fabric edge. Fold fabric in half, keeping printed sides together, and press with iron to fuse the long edges together. Let webbing cool, turn roll right-side-out. Gather fabric 3 inches from end of roll and secure with a rubber band. Fill roll with balsam potpourri to about 3 inches from unsecured end of fabric. Gather together open end of fabric and secure with second rubber band. Tie raffia strands and trim ends. Hot glue pine cones and sprigs over raffia.

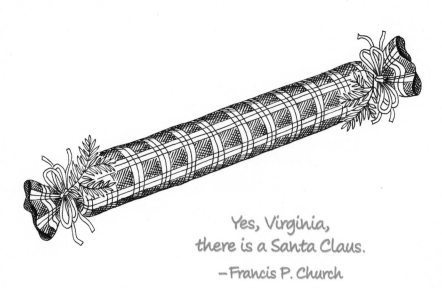

Yes, Virginia,
there is a Santa Claus.
—Francis P. Church

# ❦ Holiday Trimmings ❦

## Country-Style Spool Bows

*Tina Ledbetter*
*Moreno Valley, CA*

*A bow that's just perfect for a country Christmas!*

1 doz. one-inch wooden spools    glue gun
red and green embroidery floss    raffia

Wrap wooden spools with red and green floss; 6 spools of each color.
Using a drop of glue, secure loose end of floss on spool. Let dry.
Thread the spools onto long pieces of raffia; knotting in between spools
every few inches; set aside. So that your package will sit evenly, you
may want to measure your package first and leave off spools from the
lengths of raffia that will be on the bottom of your package. Wrap your
gift in brown kraft paper and tie several spool strands around the
package; finish by tying raffia into a bow.

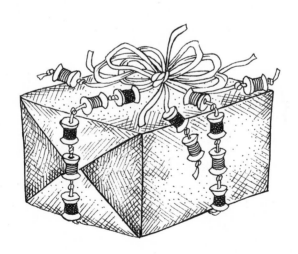

*You can also tie your spools to jute, ribbon or lengths of
homespun to add variety to your packages.*

# Layered Oatmeal-Chip Cookie Mix
*Virginia Graybill*
*Hershey, PA*

*Handwriting the instruction card gives this gift a special touch.*
*Decorate it with holiday stickers or rubber stamps, too.*

1/2 c. sugar
1/2 c. brown sugar, packed
1 c. quick-cooking oats
1 c. crispy rice cereal

1/2 c. chocolate chips
1 c. all-purpose flour
1/2 t. salt
1/2 t. baking soda

Layer first 5 ingredients in order listed, in a one-quart, wide-mouth glass canning jar. Press down firmly on each layer before adding the next ingredient. Combine flour, salt and baking soda together, mixing well. Add flour mixture on top of the chocolate chip layer. Add a gift card with the following instructions: Mix the jar ingredients with 6 tablespoons softened margarine, one beaten egg and one teaspoon vanilla extract; blending well. Roll into one-inch balls and place 2 inches apart on an ungreased cookie sheet. Bake at 350 degrees for 10 minutes. Makes 3 dozen cookies.

## Pancakes from the Pantry

*Margaret Scoresby*
*Mount Vernon, OH*

*These pancakes smell so good while they're cooking! Give with a jar of honey butter to make a really welcome gift!*

4 c. quick cooking oats
2 c. all-purpose flour
2 c. whole wheat flour
1 c. brown sugar, packed
1 c. dry milk

3 T. baking powder
2 T. cinnamon
5 t. salt
1/2 t. cream of tartar

Combine all ingredients together, mixing well. Add dry mix to an airtight container or a quart-size canning jar for gift giving. Add these instructions to your gift card: In a large mixing bowl, add 2 eggs, beat well. Gradually beat in 1/3 cup oil. Alternately add 2 cups of pancake mix and 1 cup of water to the egg mixture. Blend well. Cook pancakes on a lightly oiled griddle. Makes 10 pancakes.

*Dry mixes are always a welcome wintertime gift! Tuck the jar in a basket with a warm loaf of homemade bread and jar of honey butter.*

## Hazelnut Mocha Mix

*Mary Lou Traylor*
*Arlington, TN*

*Make your own chocolate-covered spoons to tuck inside!*

1/4 c. plus 2 T. powdered
    non-dairy creamer
1/4 c. sugar
1/4 c. hazelnut-flavored instant
    coffee
2 T. unsweetened cocoa

Combine all ingredients and mix
thoroughly. Place in a plastic
zipping bag and tuck into a
homespun bag for gift giving. Add
these serving instructions to your
gift tag: Place 2 tablespoons plus
2 teaspoons of mix in a mug, add
3/4 cup hot water.

## Homespun Jar Cookie Mix

*Mary-Ann Inlow*
*Long Beach, CA*

*A perfect gift for busy cookie lovers!*

1/4 c. walnuts, chopped
1 c. butterscotch chips
1 c. semi-sweet chocolate chips

1/2 c. shredded coconut
1 c. graham crackers, crushed

Combine ingredients in a wide-mouth glass canning jar in order listed.
Tuck in a gift card with these baking instructions: Add 1/2 cup melted
butter to graham crackers; pat evenly in the bottom of an ungreased
9"x9" baking pan. Sprinkle remaining ingredients onto graham cracker
crust, spreading evenly. Pour a 14-ounce can of sweetened condensed
milk evenly over all ingredients. Bake at 350 degrees for
30 minutes. Cool and cut into bars.

## Sweet Apple Buckle Mix

*Cheryl Bierley*
*Franklin, OH*

*A pretty market basket tied with festive ribbon nicely holds
all the ingredients for this gift mix.*

2 c. all-purpose flour
1 c. brown sugar, firmly packed
1 c. long-cooking oats
1/2 t. cinnamon
1/2 t. salt

1/4 t. nutmeg
1 c. butter
1 c. walnuts, chopped
1/3 c. cinnamon chips
4  21-oz. cans apple pie filling

In a large bowl, combine first 6 ingredients; cut in butter with a pastry blender. Stir in walnuts and cinnamon chips. Divide into 2 plastic zipping bags; store in refrigerator until ready to give as gifts. Share one bag and 2 cans of apple pie filling with these instructions: Spread both cans of apple pie filling in a lightly oiled 13"x9" baking pan. Sprinkle topping over apples and bake at 400 degrees for 20 minutes or until mixture bubbles. Serves 12.

Live each season as it passes.
—Henry David Thoreau

# Giving Gift Mixes

*Jo Ann*

*Package your homemade mixes to give as gifts! They're easy to do, and we've even included a pattern for decorating!*

★ Measure the front of a brown lunch-size bag, subtracting 4 inches from the width. Cut a length of homespun fabric the same size. Use spray adhesive on the wrong side of the fabric, then center and secure fabric to the front of your bag. Photocopy our heart, star or tree patterns and cut out. Trace pattern onto a contrasting color of homespun. Spray wrong side of fabric with spray adhesive and place on front of bag. Use a permanent black marker to draw "stitches" around the edges of the fabric. Place your plastic bag of gift mix inside the brown bag and fold top over 2 inches to the front. Use a hole punch to make 2 holes in the center of the fold and slip several lengths of raffia through the holes. Tie raffia in a bow and glue a button to the center of the bow.

★ Our picture below of a barn gift bag is easy to create! Cut a 4"x5" piece of homespun for the barn door and then cut a 1-1/2"x2-1/2" piece for the window. Following the picture below, cut the barn door fabric into 2 triangles. Lightly coat wrong sides of fabric with spray adhesive and attach to the front of the sack. Use a marker to draw lines and "stitches" around door and window. Add your gift mix inside and fold corners of bag back diagonally to create a barn roof; staple in place. Tie a bow from a long strip of fabric and glue in place over the staple.

# ❀✿ Holiday Trimmings ✿❀

## Sharing Homemade Goodies

*Vickie*

*Here are some of the ways I share my jars of homemade goodies!*

★ Spray paint a can with primer, let dry and then paint a cheerful Christmas red. Knot a strip of one-inch wide homespun around the center of the can, glue an old-fashioned button on the knot and tuck greenery around the button. Place a homespun fabric square in the can and add your jam or jelly jar.

★ Decorate your jar lids! Use your jar lid as a pattern to cut a circle of unbleached muslin. Trace our heart, star or tree patterns onto homespun fabric and attach to center of muslin circle with fusible webbing or spray adhesive. Glue a button in the center and use a marker to draw "stitches." Center muslin circle on jar lid and tighten down ring to secure and tie several lengths of raffia into a bow around the jar ring.

★ Trace our small heart or star pattern onto tracing paper, cut out. Use this pattern to cut heart or star from corrugated cardboard. Glue cardboard shape to heavy red paper and cut around shape, leaving a 1/8-inch border. Glue to top of jar lid. Tuck a sprig of greenery and small berries on the lid also.

## Country Gift Sacks

*Michelle Serrano*
*Ramona, CA*

*Give your homemade gift mixes in these country bags. Just put your favorite pancake, waffle or cookie mix in a plastic zipping bag, then tuck it inside your gift sack.*

decorative paper edger scissors
brown lunch bag
hole punch
rub-on transfer

sponge
paint
raffia or ribbon

Use decorative paper edger scissors to cut the top 1/4 inch from a brown lunch bag. Fold the top over and punch two holes, about 2 inches apart, in the center of the fold. Place a rub-on transfer onto the front of the bag. If desired, use a sponge dipped in paint and dab around transfer to create a spongeware look. Let dry thoroughly. Tuck your homemade treat inside, fold top of bag over and thread raffia or ribbon through holes in the top.

## Natural Leaf Wrap

*Coli Harrington*
*Delaware, OH*

*In early fall, collect an assortment of leaves in all shapes and sizes!*

fresh leaves
stamp pad, various shades of
   green, red, gold and copper

plastic wrap
tweezers
kraft paper

Place a leaf on the stamp pad, cover completely with a sheet of plastic wrap. Use your fingers to rub over the plastic wrap to ink the entire leaf. Gently remove the plastic and use tweezers to remove the leaf from the stamp pad. Place leaf, ink side down, onto the kraft paper and cover leaf with a scrap piece of paper. Gently rub to transfer the leaf print onto the paper. Continue stamping paper as desired, let dry.

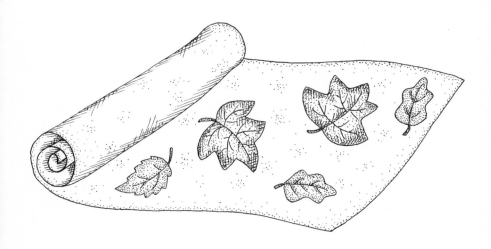

*Try using holly leaves for clever holiday wrap!*

# Embossed Cards

*Barbara Arnold*
*Toledo, OH*

*For a special gift card, just make your own!*

thin cardboard
sharp utility knife
colored paper

rounded-edge wooden craft stick
hole punch
1/8-inch wide ribbon

Photocopy the patterns below and cut out. Create your own stencil by tracing the pattern onto cardboard; cut it out with the utility knife. Place the cardboard stencil on a flat surface and lay a piece of colored paper, cut to card size, on top of the stencil. Holding the paper firmly, begin gently rubbing the paper with the craft stick. Increase the pressure until the stencil shape begins to show on the colored paper. Lift off the stencil and punch a hole in the corner. Slip ribbon through and attach to your package.

## Holiday Gift Bags

*Kathy Williamson*
*Delaware, OH*

*Easy-to-make!*

2 12"x9" pieces of felt, same color
felt scraps, variety of colors
embroidery floss
decorative paper edger scissors

glue
raffia or ribbon
jingle bells
small pine cones
rosehips

Place 2 felt pieces of the same color together and use floss to stitch closed along 2 long and one short side, with blanket or straight stitching. Use paper edger scissors to trim open edge of bag. You can also trim entire bag along outer edge, being careful not to cut too close to stitching. Create freehand hearts and stars, or photocopy our embossed card patterns, and cut shapes from felt scraps; glue to front of gift bags. Tuck gifts in bags and close with raffia or ribbon; tie jingle bells to ends. You can also glue tiny pine cones and rosehips to the bow.

Hang a kissing ball or sprig of mistletoe
in your doorway!

# Merry Gingerbread Jars

*Rebecca Franks*
*Coral Springs, FL*

*Tuck an assortment of holiday goodies inside…a wonderful housewarming or hostess gift!*

| | |
|---|---|
| gingerbread cookie recipe | 3 T. meringue powder |
| gingerbread house templates | 4 c. powdered sugar |
| thin cardboard | 6 T. warm water |
| sharp utility knife | hard candy |

Prepare gingerbread cookie recipe. Let cool. You can use templates you've purchased or make your own by cutting simple shapes from cardboard with a utility knife. Place gingerbread house templates on the gingerbread and trace around the outside edges cutting through the gingerbread. Prepare Royal Icing by combining meringue powder, powdered sugar and warm water until smooth. Use this icing to "glue" the gingerbread walls together; don't attach the roof. Let dry for 2 days. Make additional Royal Icing to decorate your cookie jar to match the hostess's home. You can pipe on lines to resemble bricks, arched windows, or double doors. Use pieces of hard candy to create a fireplace or slate roof. After the house is decorated, fill with your homebaked goodies and place the roof on top. Carefully wrap the cookie jar in plastic wrap and tie on a holiday bow.

*Deborah Stock*
*Bartonsville, PA*

My grandmother was the official pie baker. She baked two to three pies each of pumpkin, apple, mincemeat and chocolate pudding for the Christmas holiday season. I was less interested in the pies that seemed to take forever and more interested in what my grandmother would do once the final pie was complete...she would take the leftover pieces of rolled dough and place them on cookie sheets. She then lightly buttered and sprinkled the would-be pie pieces with a mixture of sugar and cinnamon. Once baked to a golden brown, they were finally ready! I always remember that moment to be the best thing about all that pie baking, although her pies were absolutely delicious. My heart was filled with admiration for my grandmother and I truly thought that she was a baking genius. As I grew older I wanted to note her personal recipes in an old cookbook she had given me. I asked for measurements, to no avail. All her recipes were from memory and taste, as true of many farming women. The most precise measurement I could write down was "a smidgen" and a general rule that the first ingredient is the largest measurement with each ingredient following being smaller. To this day I am still trying to get it right...I think it may just take a lifetime.

*Laura Cottrell*
*Payne, OH*

When I was a kid we had a room called the Fruit Room where all the canned goods were stored. In there was a counter with a large old porcelain sink in it. When it was too cold for my brother and I to go outside and play in the snow, my mother would bring snow inside and fill the sink! We could build snow castles and never have to worry about getting cold...it's a great memory I'll never forget.

# ChRiSTMAS PaST

*Lill & Jim Katzbeck*
*Sevierville, TN*

When our children were young, I wanted them to know the true meaning of Christmas, yet make it exciting for them. I wrapped up a shoebox with Christmas paper, put a slit on top of it and suggested they do good deeds daily for others. Each time they did, we could write it on a piece of paper and drop it in the box. We started at the beginning of December, and because each of our four children wanted to have the most pieces of paper in the box, they worked very hard doing good deeds. Then, on Christmas Day, they carried the box and placed it under the tree. This was a daily reminder for them to do good deeds and not to lose sight of the real meaning of Christmas.

*Salli Ross*
*Commerce Twp., MI*

I have such wonderful memories of the small town in Michigan in which I grew up. In the winter, I would wake up and run to the window hoping to see a fresh blanket of snow! Winter was so much fun! There were big sledding hills and a pond where we could ice skate. My best friend had two horses, Queenie Ann and Paint, and on snowy mornings her dad would hitch up the sleigh; complete with sleigh bells and wooly blankets, and take us for a sleigh ride all around town. What a wonderful time we had!

Volunteer to serve a holiday meal at your community shelter.

*Dawn Morrison*
*Inver Grove Heights, MN*

I learned most of my cooking talent from my Grama. One year, when I was very young, she invited me over to bake Christmas cookies. We went to the store and she let me pick out any colored sugar or decorations I wanted. We must have made at least ten kinds of cookies that night and my Grandpa enjoyed his job as taste tester! It wasn't until I was much older that my Grama told me that she was up most of that night vacuuming the cookie sprinkles and crumbs from behind the stove. I admire the love and patience she showed me, and will pass that on to my children and grandchildren.

*Monica Poole*
*Highpoint, NC*

When I was small and lived in Germany, my Mom always had a Christmas brunch and we'd have to remember a poem first in order to get a treat. It seemed like those cookies tasted so much better after learning your favorite poem! I've kept the tradition with my three daughters; but they sing a Christmas song...beautiful memories.

*Mae Blevins*
*Oak Harbor, WA*

I collect Santas and my prize one was bought in 1938, the year I married. He followed us everywhere the Navy sent us...the first on our tree, the last off. My husband and I had 57 years together, and our Santa is still around; somewhat tarnished, but so loved.

# CHRISTMAS PAST

*Sally Davis*
*Payne, OH*

I remember our second married Christmas so very well. My husband and I each had 50 cents to spend on each other. We shopped very carefully trying to get a number of items for our money. That Christmas was one of the very best...we found the best gift we could give each other was our love.

*Shauna Burns*
*Batavia, OH*

My grandmother once told me that it does not matter what a present costs, but that it is important that it truly comes from the heart. Not having very much money when we were young, she would always give her grandchildren an ornament for Christmas; sometimes store bought and sometimes handmade. When we got married, we each took our ornaments with us and now every year when we decorate the tree it brings back memories and stories from Christmases long past. After my father-in-law died my mother-in-law could not afford Christmas gifts for her many grandchildren and was very depressed. I took her to a craft show and for a very minimal amount of money she got Christmas presents that will last a lifetime, and for many generations.

*If you have treasured handwritten recipes, photocopy them to share with family. It's heart-warming to see your favorites in Grandma's handwriting.*

*Joan Morris*
*Tallahassee, FL*

I've always baked the pies for family gatherings, beginning in the 1950's. The one year that I couldn't be there, I passed along my apple and pumpkin pie recipes to my daughter-in-law, Connie. After the holiday she asked why her apple pie was neither as brown nor as crisp on top as mine. I then remembered that my addition to the recipe was something I had watched "at my mothers knee" and truly had not thought about when I copied the instructions. For the top of a two crust pie or the edge of a single crust pie, just before baking, drizzle, then spread the crust with half-and-half or evaporated milk, which is what I use, and then cover with a good shaking of sugar, or even cinnamon and sugar. Your pie will be more brown and crisp, only slightly sweeter and much more beautiful.

*Bobbylynn Williams*
*Miles City, MT*

We encourage our children to go through their toys and pick out ones that they don't play with much anymore. We then clean them up and donate them to a local shelter. We also encourage our children to choose a child's name off the Giving Tree that is roughly the same age that they are. We then let them choose a gift that they think the child would like. It is sometimes difficult for them to choose something that they would rather keep themselves, but it is a great way to teach them the joy of giving. If you do this, consider choosing a gift that the child wants, such as a toy, then you choose something that the child needs, like clothing. The parents will appreciate the needed item, while the child will love receiving something special.

# CHRISTMAS Past

*Susan Young*
*Madison, AL*

Thirty years ago, before everyone got so scattered and the family tree branched out to the point it couldn't be sketched on grocery sacks cut open and taped together, ten or fifteen close relatives would always gather for Christmas at my grandparents' wheat and cattle farm. We could always count on familiar decorations on the front of the old farm house. Grandpa always put the same ones in the same spots. I miss those big old lights...the ones that looked "misty" even if it wasn't drizzling or snowing; the ones that always worked. Those old lights were a tradition. Rumor has it my Grandmother had to "remind" Grandpa to get the lights up before the rest of us arrived; that was a tradition too; his waiting for her gentle nudging.

*Julie Miller*
*Columbus, OH*

For my family the highlight of the Christmas season has always been cutting down and decorating the Christmas tree. We would arrive at the tree farm, the air filled with music, and look at many trees before the group decision was made. The trees with the discounted orange tags have "special charm" and we frequently chose one of these. After we all took turns sawing the tree down, we would go into the shop. Once inside we would enjoy the poinsettias and wreaths but most importantly hot chocolate and popcorn by the fire. That evening while decorating the tree, according to his family's tradition, Dad would make oyster stew. He's the one who really likes the stew, but I have my one oyster per year and then decide again that I don't like oysters, but we all like the tradition. This year my parents and brother now live on the other side of the country, and I am newly married, still in Ohio. My husband and I want to continue some old family traditions, as well as make new traditions of our own; we decided this one is a keeper. Fortunately, my husband likes oysters.

Hang a festive wreath on your mailbox!

*Phyllis Peters*
*Three Rivers, MI*

As a child I longed for the Christmas holidays so I could travel a short distance to Indiana to visit my grandmother. I lived in White Pigeon, Michigan, near the state line, and enjoyed baking gingerbread men at Grandma's farmhouse and bringing back samples to my siblings. If there were enough, we made holes in the cookies to hang on the tree in the living room.

The most fun was rolling out the dough, using a shaped cookie cutter to form the little gingerbread men. Once in the cook stove oven, the cookies baked to fill the entire downstairs with an aroma that was so tempting. When Grandma Mickem took the cookies from the hot oven, she placed them on a wire rack to cool and the next batch of cut-outs were placed into the oven to bake. We mixed up frosting and decorated the cooled cookies; adding crooked lines, raisins for buttons and eyes. A little red, heart-shaped candy was used for the mouth. Red food coloring added to the frosting tinted the icing for rosy dots for cheeks.

I never tired of the annual ritual to bake gingerbread men. In fact, I carried the treasured memory to my own home for my children. It is something children never get tired of and best of all is the tasting of the completed darling figures!

Make a garland of gingerbread men! Hang it across your mantel, window or pie safe door. You'll need extra ones too...just for snacking on!

# Christmas Past

*Kathy Lam*
*Kansas City, MO*

The one thing that reminds me of Christmas long ago, is an ornament that sits upon a jewelry box near my bed. It was my favorite ornament as a child. My brother and I could not wait to get "our" ornaments out of the box each year. His ornament was a donkey and mine was an elephant. The ornaments were clear plastic with a red coloring around the details. But the most unusual part of the ornament was that it glowed in the dark; they had phosphorus in them. We would put them near a light bulb for several hours and then took them to bed at night to use as a nightlite. Often my parents had to tear them away from us after Christmas was over! They were the first ornaments out of the box and the last to be placed back into the box. The amazing thing is, they still have that warm glow after all these years!

*Yvonne Van Brimmer*
*Lompoc, CA*

The last September before Granny passed away was so special. Not sure we'd see her by Christmas, we visited her in the nursing home where she lived. We drove 200 miles with seven kids in the van! When we got there we talked about past Christmases, what I planned to do for that year, 1989, and how much I missed her fruitcake and popcorn balls; she then shared the recipes with me. Four days later I received a little note from her saying she wished she could spend Christmas with us. That same evening the nursing home called me to tell me she had peacefully passed away about the time I was reading her note. Sad? Yes, but her Christmas recipes and her love live on in so many ways. She had 93 years to share her life with others and now I'm sharing her recipes and cooking hints with my children, and soon my two grandchildren who never got to meet one of the most influential people in my life.

*Susan Maxhimer*
*Gales Ferry, CT*

Among my growing up memories of Christmas are the never-ending hunts for the perfect Christmas tree, turkey stuffing, elaborate once-a-year cookie recipes and relatives; however the memory that remains the warmest in my heart is my mother's bayberry candle.

At dusk every Christmas Eve, my mother would light a single bayberry candle in our front window. When I asked why, she explained the tradition of a light in the window to welcome the weary traveler. She told me lighting the candle was an especially important tradition for her because her mother also lit a bayberry candle in her window at that same moment of dusk. No matter how far apart they were, it was a moment of connection that brought them close, to each other and to the true meaning of Christmas. Each year as the holiday season arrived again, I would take notice as my mother tucked a bayberry candle in the Christmas package to my grandparents. I watched that candle being sent on its way and later I would watch my mother light her candle. I, too, would then let my thoughts travel to my grandmother.

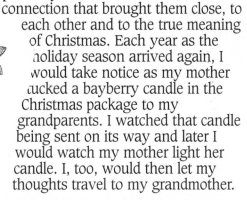

The first year I lived away from home and opened my long awaited Christmas package I found, much to my delight, a bayberry candle tucked between all the goodies. At the first moment of dusk I lit the candle. As I gazed at the flame, I imagined my mother's and my grandmother's smiles and I sent my Christmas wishes to them.

I have been away from home many years now. My grandmother passed away six years ago and Christmas seems more of a test of stamina than a joyous holiday. But when I take a moment to light my Christmas Eve candle, I always travel back to the warmth and closeness that is Christmas for me.

# Christmas Past

*Pat Ghann-Akers*
*Stanton, CA*

Each year, I make my annual trip to Michigan for a visit with my sister, Charlotte. At times, in the evening, I would be treated to an early snowfall and as Char and I sat cozy and warm, with contentedly purring cats on our laps, we would turn out the lights to watch the fat flakes drift down covering her garden with a white blanket. She would say to me, "Remember when we were kids and the first snowfall, when the ground was a perfect white blanket over the yard, inviting us to make snow angels? How much fun we had and how careful we would be to not leave too many footsteps in the snow, so we could create the perfect angel." One year, I said, "Why not?! Let's go outside and make an angel!" Two women, one 64 and one 55, out in the backyard in the middle of the night, laying down on the ground waving arms and legs to make an angel. Bones and joints cracking, having a time trying to get up off the cold ground but having the time of our lives. As I remember back and see those two angels side by side on the ground, I remember also the feeling of love between two sisters. We thoroughly enjoyed one another and the craziness. Imagine my surprise when I bought a little calender and on my sister's birthday, November 29, was the "Making a Snow Angel" picture. What a wonderful memory.

How many old recollections, and how many dormant sympathies, does Christmastime awaken!

—Charles Dickens

*Denise Rounds*
*Tulsa, OK*

When my children were just babies I made Christmas cookies each year while they slept. But as they grew to be preschool age I included them in my cookie baking sessions. They had their own aprons and measuring cups and mixing bowls. And we made snickerdoodle cookies together because they could roll a bit of dough into a ball and then roll it in a bowl of cinnamon sugar to help me.

We first baked together in 1984...I wrote a note to myself on the day we did right next to the recipe we first used. While we rolled dough and baked cookies I told them a story that my father had told me and my siblings as we grew up. As it so happened my father chose to name the main character in his stories "Snickerdoodle" so when we made the cookies with that same name, I was "forced" to tell them stories too!

The kids were spellbound as I let my imagination run wild with new adventures with this character, his friends, who were my children, and the antics he would get them into. The kids never wanted to let me end when we had finished up making our cookies...but I insisted that the stories were only for while they helped me prepare and bake the cookies. And I often had run out of ideas by that time anyway.

I had long forgotten this tradition until my daughter mentioned this week that we'd not had Snickerdoodle cookies in a long time and she proceeded to tell me one of the stories I had made up years ago; I was amazed at her memory! She still enjoys Snickerdoodles and now bakes up a batch to share with friends. Her fondest memories are not about the cookies, but about the stories we told as we baked them. They were cinnamon-sugar-scented tales that warmed her heart and soul, not just her tummy.

# Christmas Past

*Sara Burlingame*
*Ripley, WV*

One of my favorite remembrances for Christmas happened in 1985. We had built a log home and lived on a farm far removed from the city life. I had a window in the cathedral ceiling and that particular December day, it was snowing soft, airy flakes which floated slowly to Earth. It was just about dusk and the deer were starting to come out to feed. My granddaughter, Christie, and I were baking Christmas cookies and she was cutting them out as Christmas carols were playing on the radio. There is nothing spectacular about this moment, except that I was completely at peace and had no problems or worries. I often think back to that moment, especially near the holidays, and am thankful for my blessings.

*Sally White*
*Milton, VT*

I have three grandsons who have been decorating my Christmas tree since they were little guys. They come alone, no parents, and are mine for the afternoon. I always make a special treat to go along with our hot chocolate. All of the ornaments are old, many with great memories. They decorate as they please, placing ornaments where they want with no help from me. I was afraid as they grew older they wouldn't want to keep the tradition up, but they enjoy it just as much as I do.

The best gifts are tied with heartstrings.

—Anonymous

*Mary Jane Solberg*
*Jordan, MN*

Late in the afternoon of Christmas Eve, we would go to a candlelight church service in town. The pastor always read the Christmas story and we would sing our favorite carols ending with everyone singing "Silent Night" in the peaceful light of the candles and each others togetherness. Sometimes when we would open the church doors to leave, there would be a beautiful snowfall silently coming down and the only sounds to be heard were the snow in the trees and the people still in church talking. The trip home in the car was spent shivering, with not only the intense cold but the realization that the festivities would soon begin.

As soon as we got in the door, my sisters and I would run up to our bedroom, slip into our flannel pajamas Mom had sewn and put slippers on our cold feet. We'd then run past Mom, who was stirring hot cocoa on the stove and placing a few samples of holiday cookies onto a plate resting on the table, and into the living room to sit by the fire that Daddy was just getting hot and crackly. As we passed out presents to each other, we would sip our cocoa, eat our favorite cookies and open gifts. Dad would then get out his violin and play as many Christmas carols as we could think of until we were told to go to bed...Santa couldn't come until we were asleep. We each saved one of our favorite cookies for Santa's plate and Mom would fill a glass with milk; both were placed on the hearth for the long-awaited visit. Daddy would always promise that he would let the fire go cold so that Santa could safely come down the chimney.

# Giant Gingerbread Cookies

*Yvonne Van Brimmer*
*Lompoc, CA*

*For years my children have looked forward to their personal look-alike cookies tucked into their stockings!*

12-inch cookie cutters, boy and/
   or girl
gingerbread cookie recipe
3 T. meringue powder

4 c. powdered sugar
6 T. warm water
food coloring

Mix together your favorite gingerbread recipe. Because the cookie is so large, roll dough out on cookie sheet. Cut and remove any excess dough. Bake according to cookie recipe instructions and cool completely. Mix together meringue powder, powdered sugar and warm water for icing; recipe will make 3 cups of icing. Divide icing in as many bowls as you need for different colors and add food coloring. Customize each cookie with hair and eye color, glasses and their favorite clothing. Let icing dry and wrap cookies in plastic wrap until ready to eat.

# Holiday Magic for Kids

## Sock Snowman

*Jennifer Hall*
*Orleans, IN*

*For an antique look, use coffee or tea to stain sock.*

white tube sock
dried beans or birdseed
polyester fiberfill
needle and thread

fabric dye, your choice of color
scrap fabric
2 small sticks
fabric paint

Cut off the elastic cuff from the tube sock; set aside. To help snowman stand, add dried beans or birdseed to the toe; fill the remaining sock with polyester fiberfill. Stitch the top closed. To make the snowman's hat, dye the elastic cuff according to dye package directions, let dry completely. Measure 1/2 inch down from the cut edge of the elastic cuff and cinch together with needle and thread. Gently slip edges of sticks through sock for snowman's arms. Tie scrap fabric around his neck for a scarf and paint on his face.

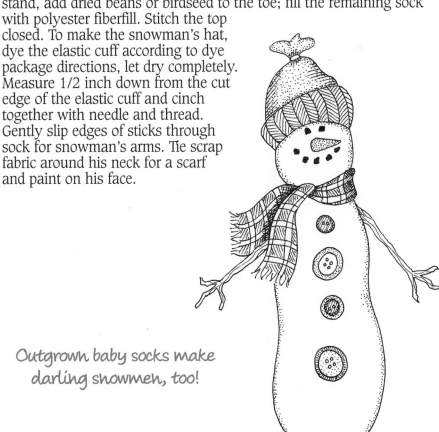

*Outgrown baby socks make darling snowmen, too!*

# Stained Glass Holiday Picture

*Judy Voster*
*Neenah, WI*

*This is an easy activity for little ones!*

holiday coloring book
glue stick

heavy cardboard
colored construction paper

Tear an uncolored page from a child's holiday coloring book and glue onto a heavy piece of cardboard. Cut or tear colored construction paper into tiny pieces. Use a glue stick to paste the tiny pieces and colors randomly on the various parts of the picture. The finished picture will look like a stained glass window mural.

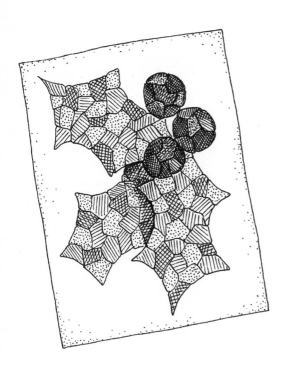

Your children can easily make these into greeting cards, invitations to a family get-together, place cards or gift tags, too. Each one will be special and Grandma and Grandpa will love receiving them!

# Holiday Magic for Kids

## Letter-to-Santa Ornament

*Tina Goodpasture*
*Meadowview, VA*

*Use your childhood memories to create letters to Santa!*

scissors
heavy cardboard
sheet from a primary writing
    tablet
white glue

black medium-point pen
glue stick
8" length of red ribbon,
    1/8" wide
hole punch

Using scissors, cut a 4"x3" rectangle from cardboard, or pencil around your favorite cookie cutter and cut out. Using your cardboard shape as a pattern, trace shape onto paper. With a black pen, let your child write a short note to Santa, keeping inside the cutting lines. Cut out shape and glue to cardboard; let dry. Using a hole punch, punch 2 holes near the top at either end of cardboard. Tie ribbon through holes for hanger.

# Handprint Coasters

*Kara Kimerline*
*Galion, OH*

*Help some little ones make this fun gift for their* Mom and Dad!

green and red tempera paint
paper plates
foam brush

heavy kraft paper
clear contact paper
small gift tags

Pour enough red paint onto a paper plate to cover a hand and a foot of your small child. Repeat this step for the green paint. Taking your foam brush, lightly paint one of your child's hands with paint. After covered, place hand onto heavy kraft paper for a hand print. Alternating colors, repeat this step for remaining hand and both feet. When paint is dry write child's name and date on them. Cover with clear contact paper and trim them in a circular shape around prints. On a small gift tag attach the following poem:

"I know my hands are little and sometimes make a mess,
So I've made for you some coasters to give your drinks a rest.
Now Merry Christmas, Mom and Dad,
It's kind of funny, can't you see?
Now I'll be helping you, by putting the mess on me!"

# Holiday Magic for Kids

## Stained Glass Candies

*Mary Lou Traylor*
*Arlington, TN*

*A beautiful ornament children and parents can make together.*

metal cookie cutters
aluminum foil
cooking oil spray
hard candy

candy sprinkles
toothpick
ribbon

Line the bottom and sides of the cookie cutter with aluminum foil. Place on a cookie sheet that's been lightly sprayed with cooking oil. Place a single layer of unwrapped hard candy into the cookie cutters. You can use whole candy pieces or crush them for a blending of colors. Place the cookie sheet in a 350 degree oven for approximately 10 minutes, or until the candy is melted. Remove from oven and add candy sprinkles; cool for 2 minutes. Carefully make a hole through the top of the candy shape with a toothpick and let your ornament cool completely. Peel off the foil and hang with a ribbon.

Put an old-fashioned train under your
tree this year!

189

# Old-Fashioned Tea for Kids

*Phyllis Peters*
*Three Rivers, MI*

*Enjoy a simple, sweet day with your children...teatime and making paper snowflakes.*

Create a simple, lasting memory for children...have a tea party. Use play dishes, serve tiny cups of milk with little cookies or a sandwich cut in little squares. Ice cream sandwiches work fine too, cut in small squares. This is a treat that will delight youngsters. Talk about "kid things" and make it a wonderful occasion. Allowed to assist with serving, a child becomes interested and likes to be helpful. It begins a delightful tradition for both the youngsters and the adults. Have a tea party soon. Promise?

# Paper Snowflakes

A paper craft children really enjoy is making snowflakes from white typing paper. I learned it in grade school many years ago and it continued to be popular after my children entered school. My great-grandchildren are just as interested in cutting designs out of paper to create a snowflake. Fold the paper in half, then again and again. Using blunt scissors, cut out tiny circles, triangles and notches; unfold. Round the corners. See how many different kinds a child can design. The beautiful designs should be allowed a space on the refrigerator, pinned to a curtain or taped in a window to be enjoyed by all.

## Snowman Christmas Treat Pots

*Christi Miller*
*New Paris, PA*

*A really clever gift filled with favorite candy!*

6 to 7-inch clay pot
acrylic paint in white, ivory,
    black and orange
sponge
acrylic sealer
homespun fabric
hot glue gun and glue sticks

greenery
berries
polyester fiberfill
plastic wrap
wrapped candies or cookies
knit cap
buttons

Basecoat inside and outside of clay pot with white acrylic paint; dry completely. Sponge paint ivory acrylic paint on top of the white paint; let dry. On the front of the pot, paint a snowman's face. When paint has thoroughly dried, spray entire pot with acrylic sealer. Tie a strip of homespun fabric around the base for his scarf and hot glue into place. Place a handful of polyester fiberfill into the bottom of pot. Line the inside with plastic wrap and fill with wrapped candies or cookies. Stitch some buttons on the knit cap, glue on some greenery and red berries and place cap over the rim of the pot.

Snuggle up
with your
little ones
under a warm
cozy blanket
and watch the
snow fall.

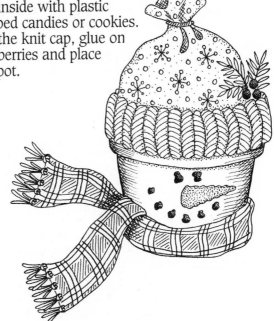

191

# Play-Dough

*Denise Rounds*
*Tulsa, OK*

*What child doesn't like playing with dough? Kids will enjoy*
*making these soft pretzels in any shape.*

1 pkg. active yeast
1-1/2 c. warm water
1 t. salt
1 T. sugar

4 c. all-purpose flour
1 egg white, beaten
Garnish: rock salt

Soften yeast with water. Add salt, sugar and flour. Mix together until a dough is formed. Let the children knead and shape the dough into pretzels, candy canes or wreaths and place on a floured surface. Lay the shapes they form onto a greased cookie sheet. Brush with egg white, sprinkle with salt and bake in a 425 degree oven for 15 minutes.

# Peanut Butter Play-Dough

*Stacy Weichert*
*Moorhead, MN*

*Have fun making all sorts of shapes...it's edible!*

1 c. peanut butter
1-1/2 c. powdered milk

3 T. honey

Mix together and play! Does not keep, discard when done.

# Holiday Magic for Kids

## Paper Sack Gingerbread Man

*June Weddle*
*Arlington, TX*

*A fun and easy project...for parents and kids!*

2 brown paper sacks
pencil
acrylic paint
brushes
polyester fiberfill

glue
pinking shears
clothes pins

Take apart 2 brown paper sacks. Press with a hot iron to remove as many wrinkles as possible. Lay sacks together, printed sides facing each other. Using a pencil, freehand a gingerbread figure onto one square of brown paper sack, add a 1/2 inch to your drawing. Around the paper sack edges, away from your drawing, staple the 2 pieces of sack together. Following your pencil marks, sew around pattern edges with sewing machine. Cut around edge with pinking shears. Use acrylic paint to decorate gingerbread man; set side to dry. When thoroughly dry, carefully cut a slit in the middle of back being very careful not to go through front of the gingerbread man. Lightly stuff with polyester fiberfill. To hide slit in back, cut another gingerbread man the size of the one you are working on minus the pinking line. Glue over back of doll, securing with clothes pins until glue dries. This will give you a nice back to paint on if desired.

# Gifts for the Birds

*Susan Young*
*Madison, AL*

*It may take a few days for the birds to discover their gifts...but they will!*

4 lbs. suet
1 c. peanut butter
3 to 4 c. corn meal
5 c. birdseed

cranberries, chopped
mesh bags
spool of jute

Melt suet in deep pan over low heat. Do not leave pan unattended. Using care, divide suet between 2 large bowls. To each, add 1/2 cup peanut butter, approximately 2 cups corn meal and 2-1/2 cups bird seed. Mix well. Add cranberries. If mixture is too soft, add more seed and corn meal. Place mixture into mesh bags. Let cool in cold garage or on porch. Using jute, tie bags from tree branches.

Don't forget to leave plenty of fresh water for the birds in wintertime. Remember to break the ice, too!

## Homemade Cookie Cards

*Terri Demidovich*
*Charleston, SC*

*Spend a snowy day making these personalized cards!*

your favorite sugar cookie recipe
3 T. meringue powder
4 c. powdered sugar
6 T. warm water

red and green food coloring
small brush or pastry bag
sprinkles or colored sugar

Prepare your favorite sugar cookie dough according to the recipe. While dough is chilling, prepare Royal Icing by blending together meringue powder, powdered sugar and warm water until smooth. Cover and set aside. Remove chilled dough from refrigerator, divide in half, and roll one half into a 10"x9" rectangle. Using a pastry wheel, trim around the outer edge of the rectangle; then divide rectangle into 9 equal portions. Separate the "cookie cards" from one another and place on a foil-lined baking sheet. Repeat with remaining dough. Bake cookies according to recipe directions, cool on baking sheet and then place on wire racks to cool completely. To decorate cookies, divide Royal Icing into 3 separate bowls, tint 2 of the bowls with food coloring, leave the third one white. You can thin down some of the icing with a few drops of water to paint a thin coat of color on the cookies. Use a pastry bag with a small tip to write your holiday greetings on each cookie. Decorate with colored sugar or sprinkles and set aside to dry completely. To add variety to your cookies, you can add food coloring to the dough, before rolling out, or use small cookie cutters to cut designs into unbaked cookies and fill the opening with crushed hard candy.

# Ice Cream Ornament

*Lisa Watkins*
*Gooseberry Patch*

*This ornament still hangs on my parents' tree every Christmas.*

clear spray varnish
craft glue
ice cream cones
plain glass ball ornaments to fit
    cones

brown and white acrylic paint
plastic spoons
sprinkles

Set cones upside down on plastic outdoors and spray lightly with 2 coats of clear spray varnish. Let dry. Glue ornament into the cone with hanger on top. Thin paint with water. Spoon paint over the ornament allowing it to drip over the top like sauce. Before it dries, drop sprinkles over ornament. Let dry.

Use all shapes of ice cream cones for
this ornament, even big waffle cones
are fun! If you want to give these ornaments as gifts,
pack them in a colorful plastic ice cream tub filled
with lots of tissue paper for protection.

# Photo Box

*Tami Bowman*
*Marysville, OH*

*Childhood birthdays, fishing trips or pictures taken Christmas morning all make perfect photos for this keepsake!*

acrylic paint, assorted colors
paper maché box
2 to 3 foam brushes

matte finish decoupage medium
decorative paper edger scissors
color photocopies of photos

Paint paper maché box with color of your choice inside and out. Let dry for at least 2 hours and paint again. Let dry. Cut photocopies of photos with fun-shaped edger scissors. Get a rough idea of how you'll arrange your photos on the box. Using a foam brush, brush a light coat of decoupage medium on the back of the photo and place on the box, using your fingers to smooth it out. Once you've covered the box with photos, paint over the entire box with decoupage sealer. It will look really heavy and cloudy, but don't worry it dries clear. Let box dry thoroughly, at least 2 hours. Seal with as many coats of decoupage medium as you need to completely fill in the "ridges" around the edges of photos. Usually 2 or 3 coats. Let dry and cure for one or 2 days before putting lid on the box.

Once your photo boxes are complete, stack several together and tie with a wide bow...a gift full of memories!

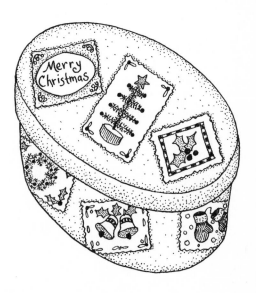

# HoMe Spun HaNdiworks

## Evergreen Bundles

Mary Lou Traylor
Arlington, TN

*A welcome holiday gift that will be enjoyed all winter long! Add heart-felt "ornaments" to make it special…baby booties, a pair of Grandma's gloves, a handmade stocking, tiny baby socks, dried flowers from a special occasion or store-bought ornaments that reflect special hobbies.*

variety of evergreen sprigs
rubber band
1/8" wide ribbon

1/2" wide holiday ribbon
ornaments

Gather stems together and secure with the rubber band. Make a loop to hang your evergreen bundle by wrapping a length of 1/8" wide ribbon twice around the top of the bundle, securely tie in a knot on the back of your bundle. About 3 inches up, tie another knot, then tie remaining length into a bow. Cover the rubber band with the 1/2" wide ribbon and tie a bow on the front of your bundle. Tuck a small wire ornament hook to the ribbon or rubberband underneath the bow and attach your ornament.

Christmas comes but once a year,
and when it comes it brings good cheer!
—Mother Goose

# Farmhouse Signs

*Mel Wolk*
*St. Peters, MO*

*These little signs may be personalized with a name or old-fashioned greeting...Wooly Mittens, Sleighbells or Hearth & Home.*

1"x4" board cut into 6-inch
   lengths
acrylic paint
scrap paper
alphabet stencils
stencil brushes
paint brush

medium eye screws
pliers
sandpaper
clear polyurethane spray
20 gauge blackened wire
raffia or homespun ribbon
miscellaneous ornaments

If desired, distress wood by pounding with hammer and hammering impressions of nails, screws and chains onto surface. Paint front and back of board with one solid base color. Two coats may be required for coverage. Let dry. Stencil saying or name onto scrap paper to make sure the words fit and to adjust spacing. Stencil saying onto board. Dark country-style colors stenciled with white or cream letters look great. When completely dry, sand edges to get a slightly worn look. Spray with the clear polyurethane spray and let dry. Insert eye screws along the top edge about 2 inches from the edges of the sign. Place one end of the blackened wire through one hole about 3 inches and twist to hold. Repeat on the other side, adjusting length of wire to desired length; twist together the other side. Attach a raffia or homespun bow, buttons, jingle bells or ornaments for decoration.

# HoMe Spun HaNdiworkS

## Helping Hands Apron

*Kimberley Fisher*
*Cambridge, NY*

*My children's grandparents live far away, so we made these as holiday gifts. It's a nice way for them to feel as though the children are there when they are doing the holiday baking and crafts!*

foam brushes
fabric paint

white apron
fine-point permanent marker

Use foam brushes to lightly apply paint to childrens' hands. Help the children firmly place their hands onto apron, then gently remove. Repeat as many times as you wish. When paint has thoroughly dried, use a marker to write names and ages next to the handprints.

Even little footprints would be darling on this apron!

# Punched Tin Pie Plates

*Vickie*

*Give this hand-crafted gift to a dear friend...tuck in a recipe card sharing your favorite pie recipe!*

9" aluminum pie pan              hammer
masking tape                          awl

Photocopy patterns, enlarging as needed. Center pattern inside of pie pan and tape in place to secure. Place pan on a protected surface and lightly punch pattern markings with hammer and awl, being careful not to punch completely through pie pan. When all dots have been lightly punched, remove pattern.

The road to a friend's house is never long.

—Anonymous

# HomeSpun Handiworks

## Patterns for Punched Tin Pie Plates

# Wintertime Wall Hanging

*Sara Tatham*
*Plymouth, NH*

*Hang these in the kitchen or tuck into a gift basket for a friend.*

16"x11" homespun dish towel
fusible web
10"x8" square of muslin

fine-point permanent marker
homespun fabric squares
buttons

Hem the raw edges, if any, of your dishtowel. Using fusible web, iron muslin square in the center of the dishtowel. With your marker, letter a seasonal recipe onto the muslin square…Snow Ice Cream would be fun, or share your favorite winter stew or bread recipe. Cut snowflakes, fir trees, snowmen or hearts from your fabric squares and iron on with fusible web. Add buttons to the corners for a homespun touch.

Snow Ice Cream
1c. heavycream
Sugar
Vanilla extract
4c. perfectly
clean snow

Share your favorite family recipes on these
wall hangings...great for a new bride!

# HoMe Spun HaNdiworKS

## Memory Quilt

*Denise Rounds*
*Tulsa, OK*

When my daughter was young, I spent many a holiday season sewing her sweet dresses. It was a joyful labor and she loved it as much as I did. She and I chose the patterns, fabrics and buttons together each time she needed a new dress. But as she became a teenager she didn't care to have homemade dresses anymore. She still loved the dresses of her past and didn't want to part with them, so I pondered on what to do. We had kept all her "mom-made" dresses so I could pick through them and choose the ones she wanted to keep for her own children one day. The remaining ones I cut apart, pressed and cut into 3-inch squares. I found a simple quilt pattern and set to making a comforter for her. The pretty florals and the sweet pastels all worked together to make a wonderful top that I backed with white and sandwiched with 3 layers of fluffy batting. I tied the quilt with pretty pink, thin satin ribbon. And then I gave it to her as winter arrived the 13th year of her life. We now have a memory quilt that she absolutely adores! It's fluffy, light and gives her truly warm memories of sweet dresses, holidays and childhood. She never neglects to explain to her friends who admire this comforter that it's from her many dresses and she recalls each one with a smile while her friends "oooh" and "ahhhh." It's a gift from my heart that will be treasured for years and remembered forever.

*Your kids will enjoy dreaming of Christmas snuggled under their favorite warm quilt.*

# Cookie Pull Toys

*Sandy Spayer*
*Jeromesville, OH*

*Have fun with a variety of animal-shaped cookies!*

cut-out cookie recipe
3 T. meringue powder
4 c. powdered sugar
6 T. warm water
food coloring

small paint brushes
round peppermint candies
graham crackers
licorice whips

Mix together your favorite
cookie cut-out dough. On a
lightly floured surface, roll
dough to 1/8-inch thickness.
Use 2 to 3-inch animal-shaped
cookie cutters and cut out an
equal number of cookies,
making sure to have a pair of
each animal. Transfer cookies
to an ungreased baking sheet,
remembering to turn over half of
the animals so that they are facing
the opposite direction. Bake according
to recipe instructions. Cool. Combine

meringue powder, powdered sugar and water to make icing. Combine
1-1/2 cups of icing and one tablespoon water in a small mixing bowl.
Add additional water until icing is of a brushing consistency. Divide
icing into individual small bowls, using food coloring to tint each to
desired color. Using a small paint brush, paint animals. Let dry for
one to 2 hours, or until icing is completely dry. Place the remaining
white icing into a decorating bag fitted with a tip and pipe icing on
the backs of the matching animals to "glue" them together; let dry for
30 minutes. Ice 2 peppermint candies together for a wheel, making
4 wheels for each graham cracker; let dry for 30 minutes, then attach
a wheel to each corner of the graham cracker. Turn graham cracker
over and attach a length of licorice for a pull handle. Let wheels and
handle dry for 30 minutes. Secure animals with icing to the top of the
graham cracker and let dry for 30 minutes. Repeat for all animals.

# HoMe Spun HaNdiworks

## Stenciled Lamp Shades

*Crystal Lappie*
*Worthington, OH*

*Do you have a friend who has a favorite collection of angels, cats or Santas? Choose a special stencil just for her!*

plain white lamp shade
acrylic paints
paint brush
paper plate

small round sponges
paper towels
stencils

Paint your lamp shade a solid color. After the paint is completely dry, position your stencil where you'd like the stencil design and secure it with masking tape. Place a small amount of paint on a paper plate. Dip round sponge in paint, blotting excess onto paper towels. Gently press sponge into open areas of stencil, changing colors as needed. After you have painted the design, gently lift the tape and stencil off your shade and let dry.

*Stencil designs on your lampshades and change them with the seasons!*

# Votive Jar Lamp

*Jennifer Jordan*
*Westerville, OH*

*Line these on your steps or along a garden path.*

quart-size glass canning jar
acrylic paint
paint brushes
stencil brushes
stencils

acrylic sealer
votive holder
votive candle
ribbon or raffia

Thoroughly wash and dry a glass canning jar. Spray with a solid color of acrylic paint; let dry. Paint or stencil designs on the outside of your jar...snowmen, evergreen trees, stars or snowflakes for a winter scene. When paint is dry, thoroughly coat with acrylic sealer. Slip votive holder inside of jar opening so it fits snugly at the jar rim, tuck candle inside holder. Tie a ribbon or raffia bow around the jar neck.

Place several jar lamps on the steps to your porch. They'll cast a soft glow and light the path to your doorway. You can also partially fill several jars with sand and set a tea light inside. Line them along your driveway for holiday luminarias.

# HomeSpun Handiworks

## Handmade Soap

*Patricia Husek*
*Saint Joseph, MI*

*Create your own special scent by trying different herb blends.*

1 bar of snowy-white soap
dried rosemary, lavender or
    lemon balm
lemon, lime or orange peel

scented oil
warm water
tulle raffia or brown paper
ribbon

Finely chop soap into thin slivers with a sharp knife. Add as much or as little of the herbs and citrus peel as you'd like. Heat soap mixture in a microwave-safe bowl for one to 2 minutes or until soap becomes fluffy. Remove from microwave and immediately add a few drops of scented oil. When cool, add approximately one tablespoon of warm water and quickly mold with your hands. You'll need to work very quickly and use the liquid and hand pressure to press all the ingredients together. Roll into a ball. Wrap in netting, raffia or brown paper and tie with a length of ribbon.

Pile your handmade soaps into a basket; add some bath salts, a soft fluffy towel and a tape of relaxing music...a great gift for a busy mom!

# Muslin Snowmen

*Ann Magner*
*New Port Richey, FL*

*Let snowmen decorate your mantel all winter long!*

| | |
|---|---|
| drawing paper | fabric paint, black and white |
| 1/4 yard muslin | twigs |
| polyester fiberfill | hot glue gun and glue |
| sand | toothpick |
| sandwich bag | orange polymer clay |
| cardboard | cloves |
| paintbrushes | water-based varnish |

On paper, draw a freehand snowman, add 3/8-inch seam allowance and cut out. Fold muslin piece in half; trace paper snowman on to muslin and cut out 2 pieces of fabric. Pin pieces together and hand or machine stitch; leaving openings at the bottom and on each side for arms. Gently stuff snowman head and body with polyester fiberfill. Pour sand into a sandwich bag and tie bag tightly closed. Place bag into base of snowman and stuff polyester fiberfill around bag until firm. Trace snowman base on cardboard and cut out. Cut a scrap piece of muslin that's slightly larger than the cardboard, wrap around cardboard and glue edges under. With raw edges on top, glue cardboard base to bottom of snowman. Paint snowman with white fabric paint; let dry. Insert and glue twigs in sides for arms. Break toothpick into a small piece, form piece of clay into a nose and place on toothpick. Bake clay according to package directions. Insert nose through fabric and glue into place. Paint mouth and eyes with black paint dots, glue cloves for buttons. Varnish entire snowman; allow to completely dry.

# HoMe Spun HaNdiWorkS

## Spool Ornaments

*Heather Alexander*
*Lacey, WA*

*I like to make a new ornament each Christmas; this is
a thoughtful gift for the seamstress or quilter on your list!*

11 thread spools
green and brown embroidery
   floss
glue gun and glue

buttons
brass star charm
gold cord

Wrap 10 empty thread spools evenly with green embroidery floss.
Wrap one spool with brown embroidery floss. Make a pyramid out of
the green spools, gluing them together at the tops and bottoms of the
spools. Glue the brown spool to the middle of the bottom to create the
tree trunk. Add small buttons to the front of the tree to resemble
ornaments, and a brass charm tops the tree as a star. Thread the
gold cord into the hole in the top spool for hanging.

Hang spool ornaments along with thimbles, buttons and
small bobbins on a tree in your sewing room.

# Homespun Stockings

*Corrine Lane*
*Marysville, OH*

*Create special homemade stockings!*

felt, flannel or homespun
natural batting
embroidery thread

buttons, bells or patches
length of homespun or ribbon

Using a photocopier, enlarge or reduce stocking pattern to desired size.
Trace pattern onto felt, flannel or homespun and cut 2 stocking pieces
out. Using a sewing machine or
blanket stitch, stitch sides together
leaving top open. Tie off any loose
threads. Enlarge or reduce cuff
pattern to fit stocking size; cut
out pattern. Fold batting in half
lengthwise and place on fold line
of cuff pattern; cut out fabric.
Stitch batting cuff to the top of the
stocking. Aligning the short ends of
the cuff with the back seam of the
stocking, tie off any loose threads.
Give your stocking an old-fashioned
feel; add buttons, tiny bells or
homespun patches. To make a loop
for hanging, add a length of
homespun or ribbon to the top back
seam, tie loose ends in a bow.

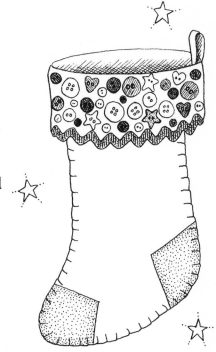

Make stockings from outgrown flannel shirts. You'll have
sweet memories whenever you look at them.

# ℋoℳeℒpun ℋanⅆiwoℛⅎS

## Pattern for Homespun Stockings

Batting Fold Line

# Broomstraw Stars

*Judy Voster*
*Neenah, WI*

*This is the kind of project that reminds me of "the good old days" when Christmas decorations were made lovingly by hand and passed down in the family. Now you can make these old-fashioned stars and have a special keepsake to pass down in your family.*

whiskbroom                     thread
white glue                     colored string

Each star is made up of 5 bundles of broomstraw. To make a bundle, clip or break 10 to 12 straws from the whiskbroom. Holding the straws together, dab a bit of glue around them close to one end. Wrap thread around the straws and over the glue several times. Repeat at the opposite end of the bundle. Make 5 bundles. Lay the bundles in a star shape with ends overlapping. Place a drop of glue at each intersection. Place a heavy book over the star. At each intersection tie a knot with the colored string, place a drop of glue and tie a second knot. Star should slip right onto a branch, no hanger needed.

You can make old-fashioned twig stars using the same instructions as for broomstraw stars.

# HomeSpun Handiworks

## Heirloom Mirror

*Carina Baker*
*Wayland, NY*

*Old postcards, special letters and family photos are lovely displayed in this old-fashioned frame.*

newspaper
framed mirror
postcards, letters or pictures
furniture stripper

steel wool pad
glass cleaner
paper towels

Before you begin, be sure to work in a well-ventilated room. Lay newspaper around the area that you will be working. Remove mirror from frame and set frame aside. Tape picture, letter or postcard to the front side of the mirror; wrong side facing you. Turn mirror over, so the silver finish is facing up and apply furniture stripper to the entire area, wait until surface bubbles and carefully wipe away with paper towels; discard. When all the silver backing is removed apply more stripper to the mirror backing and wait about 10 to 15 minutes. Using the steel wool pad, scrub the mirror part away until you see your picture coming through the glass, continue to spray the stripper only in the areas that you want to see the picture through; leave it cloudy around the edges. After you've removed enough silver so that all the picture you want to see is showing through, untape the picture from the front. Clean front and back with glass cleaner. Attach the picture or postcard to the back of the mirror this time so the picture shows through the area you stripped away and the mirror surrounds the picture. Place the mirror back in the frame, securing well.

# Glass Memory Bulb

*Cindy Baum*
*Helena, MT*

*I like to remember when special occasions happen, and this glass bulb painting is great for recording family memories.*

clear glass or acrylic bulbs          transparent glass paint
ultra fine point permanent pen

Clean bulb and dry carefully. Using permanent pen, write in a circular motion, beginning at the top, the various things your family did throughout the year...your child's "firsts", your favorite movie that year, or the vacation you took. Continue writing sentence after sentence or leave a space after a sentence and with the glass paint draw a tree, a small pine bough or holly leaf. When you finish, use another color of ink and write the year. You can also help your children make a bulb of their own special memories of that year.

Have family and friends sign a memory bulb for
a college student far from home.

# HomeSpun Handiworks

## Grandma's Hug Quilt

*Mel Wolk*
*St. Peters, MO*

*This could be a wonderful gift from your family that everyone works on throughout the year. Small children can stack and lay out squares. Older children can cut squares and stitch with adult supervision and everyone gets to make handprints!*

outgrown clothing
scissors
thread
sewing machine
white or unbleached muslin
additional fabric as needed

fabric paint
foam brush
embroidery thread
quilt batting
coordinating fabric for backing
heavy thread for tying

Cut children's outgrown clothing, cottons and blends only, into equal-size squares. Place pieces together in a simple patchwork quilt top, adding additional fabric if needed. In all 4 corners add a square of muslin and machine stitch the squares together to form a quilt top. Carefully brush each person's hand with fabric paint and gently press handprints in the muslin corners, or on other fabric squares. When paint has dried, embroider names and dates in the squares. Layer quilt batting between quilt top and fabric backing, add a simple fabric strip edging. Quilt or hand tie into a fluffy warm quilt to "wrap Grandma in hugs" on cold winter nights.

Your hug quilt can also be sized down to become cozy lap-size.

# Canning Jar Lamp

*Mary Murray*
*Gooseberry Patch*

*A fun, old-fashioned way to light up your holiday.*

awl
quart-size glass canning jar with
    lid and ring
fiberglass wick
ceramic lamp oil adapter
unscented pine cones, cinnamon
    sticks, rosehips, dried orange
    peel, whole cloves, star anise

clear lamp oil
glass hurricane, same diameter
    as mouth of canning jar
homespun ribbon or curly wire

Using an awl, gently tap a hole in the center of the canning jar lid.
Insert wick through bottom of lid. Set lamp oil adapter, available at
candle shops, on top of hole and feed wick through it also. Fill a clean,
dry canning jar with a variety of dried items; cover completely with
lamp oil. Lay ring on top of jar, gently pushing wick into oil and dried
items. Tighten lid down with ring. Slip glass hurricane over lid and
ring. Decorate your lamp by adding a length of homespun around
the jar neck or curly wire and a rusty tin star.

*Paint or stencil a winter
scene on your glass canning
jar before you fill it! Dip a
sponge into paint, blot off
the excess and decorate your
jar. When the paint's dry,
coat the jar with a sealer.*

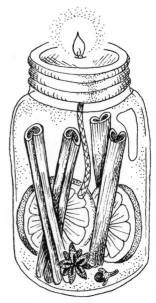

# Home Spun Handiworks

## Measuring Spoon Ornaments

*Cheryl Bierley*
*Franklin, OH*

*This ornament will be perfect on your kitchen tree!*

set of measuring
  spoons
acrylic paint

matte finish sealer
ornament hook

Thoroughly clean and dry a set of measuring spoons. Turning spoon over so rounded part is facing you, paint white and let dry. With paint, add eyes, nose and mouth. When completely dry, spray with sealer. Slip hook through hole in top of spoon to hang.

## Snow Candles

*Joyce Young*
*Gunnison, CO*

*The small flames cast beautiful reflections against the snow to light a path or decorate porch steps!*

snow

tea lights

Roll snowballs 7 inches in diameter. Using a spoon or ice cream scoop, hollow out a hole in the top that goes through the snowball, almost to the bottom. When dark, place small tea light candles into the snowballs and light them.

Make a snowball campfire for your snowmen! Roll two dozen snowballs; stack them in a circle. Tuck votives inside to create a glow!

# index

## APPETIZERS

Brown Sugar Ham Balls, 30
Cheryl's Holiday Cheese Ball, 39
Chicken Fingers & Honey Mustard, 35
Cream Cheese Fruit Dip, 34
Cream Cheese Pastry, 32
Dried Beef Spread, 31
Garlic Dip, 32
Mixed Fruit Ball, 34
Mom's BLT Dip, 37
Pepperoni Spread, 37
Pine Cone Cheeseball, 33
Reuben Dip, 36
Sweet Red Pepper Dip, 38

## BEVERAGES

Apple Creamy, 41
Colorado Cocoa, 21
Hot Mulled Punch, 43
Hot Vanilla, 42
Old-Fashioned Egg Nog, 42
Old-Fashioned Russian Tea, 22
Santa Claus Milk, 40
Wassail, 43
White Christmas Punch, 40
Wintertime Spice Tea, 11

## BREADS

Butterhorn Rolls, 80
Granny's Biscuits, 83
Holiday Cloverleaf Rolls, 68
Honeybee Rolls, 74
Mamau's Biscuits, 85
Never-Fail Dinner Rolls, 88
Oatmeal Molasses Bread, 71
Sourdough Bread Stuffing, 48
Sourdough Country Loaf, 77

## BREAKFAST

Apple Puff Flapjacks, 6
Applesauce Pancakes, 15
Baked Peach Pancake, 24
Blueberry French Toast, 7
Buttermilk-Raisin Buns, 18
Cherry Coffeecake, 14
Christmas Morn Sausage Rolls, 9
Country Scramble, 26
Dutch Babies, 17
Egg & Sausage Bake, 27
Fieldstone Farm Popovers, 8
French Toast Waffles, 16
Mom's Granola, 10
Old-Fashioned Baked Eggs, 12
Raspberry Coffeecake, 25
Raspberry Muffins, 19
Sausage Quiche, 13
Sour Cream Breakfast Coffeecake, 20
Stuffed French Toast, 23
Warm Country Waffles, 28

## BUTTERS, DRESSINGS & SYRUPS

Apple Cider Syrup, 15
Cinnamon, Pecan & Honey Syrup, 28
Pilgrim Sauce, 53
Raspberry Vinaigrette, 59
Strawberry Butter, 16

## CASSEROLES

Cabbage & Pork Chop Casserole, 93
Farmstead Pumpkin Casserole, 52
Potato & Spinach Casserole, 50

## DESSERTS

Apple Crumble Pie, 127
Apple Crunch, 132
Apple Dumpling Roll, 147
Apple Raisin Cobbler Pie, 128
Candy Cane Thumbprints, 123
Caramel Apple Crisp, 138
Chocolate Layer Pie, 143
Christmas Butter Fudge, 146
Cinnamon Pudding Cake, 134
Cream Cheese Pound Cake, 136
Fondant, 142
German Chocolate Cake, 129
Gingerbread Men, 148
Ginger Cookies, 126
Ginger Creams, 124
Grandma's Blackberry Cobbler, 120
Great Grandma's Christmas Cookies, 140
Hard Tac Candy Treats, 128
Hot Milk Sponge Cake, 137
Lebkuchen, 121
Lemon Chess Pie, 130
Maple Meltaways, 125
Mary's Christmas Cookies, 135
Molasses Gingersnap Cookies, 141
Old-Fashioned Cream Pie, 133
Old-Fashioned Spicy Pumpkin Pie, 139
Orange Mallow Pie, 136
Peanut Butter Fudge, 131
Praline Banana Cake, 145
Sugar Cream Pie, 122
Sugar Plums, 144
Sugared Apples, 125

## MAINS

Baked Ham in a Blanket, 108
Brown Sugar Ham Steaks, 101
Chicken with Biscuit Topping, 114
Chicken & Dumplings, 111
Chicken & Strudel, 98
Classic Sauerbraten, 115
Country Chicken Pie, 103
Country Glazed Ham, 113
Country-Fried Steak, 96
Country-Style Ribs, 91
Garden Meat Loaf, 99
Granny's Pot Roast, 118

# index

Hearty Beef Brisket, 109
Holiday Ham Loaf, 94
Homemade Chicken & Egg Noodles, 106
Honey Roasted Pork Loin, 102
Maple Roasted Chicken, 95
Mom's Chicken & Dressing, 90
Mom's Lasagna, 100
Nancy's Turkey Pie, 92
Oven Baked Barbecue Beef, 104
Peppered Sirloin Steak, 105
Pork & Raspberry Sauce, 112
Quick & Easy Fried Chicken, 117
Stuffed Beef Tenderloin, 116
Stuffed Pepper Cups, 107
Sunday Night Supper, 97
Sweet-and-Spicy Glazed Turkey, 110

## SALADS

Ambrosia Waldorf Salad, 58
Creamy Broccoli & Cauliflower Salad, 56
Crunchy Salad with Dill Dressing, 57
Dark Cherry Salad, 58
Honey-Carrot Salad, 60
Mandarin Orange Salad, 59
Marinated Carrot Salad, 55
Mozzarella & Tomato Salad, 61
Old-Fashioned Coleslaw, 54
Sour Cream Potato Salad, 62

## SOUPS

Bean & Pasta Soup, 70
Beef & Barley Vegetable Soup, 81
Beef, Vegetable & Macaroni Soup, 79
Brown Rice Turkey Soup, 78
Carrot & Potato Soup, 73
Christmas Eve Sauerkraut Soup, 86
Cream of Fresh Tomato Soup, 76
Grandma's Chili, 72
Grannie's Basil Soup, 64
Ham & Bean Soup, 67
Hearty Vegetable Soup, 82
Old-Fashioned Chicken Soup, 84
Spinach-Chicken Noodle Soup, 66
Stew with Winter Vegetables, 87
Wash Day Stew, 65
Wild Rice Soup, 69
Winter Chicken Stew, 75

## VEGETABLES

Baked Butternut Squash & Apples, 51
Baked Yams with Nutmeg Butter, 44
Christmas Cauliflower, 46
Golden Mashed Potatoes, 47
Grandma Margie's Scalloped Corn, 49
Vanilla-Glazed Sweet Potatoes, 45

## CRAFTS

Balsam Draft Stoppers, 156
Broomstraw Stars, 214

Canning Jar Lamp, 218
Cookie Pull Toys, 206
Country Gift Sacks, 164
Country-Style Spool Bows, 157
Edible Cookie Bowl, 155
Embossed Cards, 166
Evergreen Bundles, 199
Farmhouse Signs, 200
Giant Gingerbread Cookies, 184
Gift-Filled Jar Candle, 153
Gifts for the Birds, 194
Giving Gift Mixes, 162
Glass Memory Bulb, 216
Grandma's Hug Quilt, 217
Grocery Bag Wrapping Paper, 152
Handmade Gift Tags, 154
Handmade Soap, 209
Handprint Coasters, 188
Hazelnut Mocha Mix, 160
Heirloom Mirror, 215
Helping Hands Apron, 201
Holiday Gift Bags, 167
Homemade Cookie Cards, 195
Homespun Jar Cookie Mix, 160
Homespun Stockings, 212
Ice Cream Ornaments, 196
Layered Oatmeal-Chip Cookies, 158
Letter-to-Santa Ornament, 187
Measuring Spoon Ornaments, 219
Memory Quilt, 205
Merry Gingerbread Jars, 168
Muslin Snowmen, 210
Natural Leaf Wrap, 165
Old-Fashioned Tea for Kids, 190
Pancakes from the Pantry, 159
Paper Sack Gingerbread Man, 193
Paper Snowflakes, 190
Peanut Butter Play-Dough, 192
Photo Box, 198
Play-Dough, 192
Punched Tin Pie Plates, 202
Sharing Homemade Goodies, 163
Snow Candles, 219
Snowman Christmas Treat Pots, 191
Sock Snowman, 185
Sponge-Painted Christmas Tins, 150
Spool Ornaments, 211
Stained Glass Candies, 189
Stained Glass Holiday Picture, 186
Stenciled Lamp Shades, 207
Stenciled Gift Wrap, 151
Stenciled Tissue Paper, 151
Sweet Apple Buckle Mix, 161
Votive Jar Lamp, 208
Wintertime Wall Hanging, 204

# Find Gooseberry Patch wherever you are!
# www.gooseberrypatch.com

Email

## Call us toll-free at 1·800·854·6673

---

## U.S. to Metric Recipe Equivalents

### Volume Measurements

| | |
|---|---|
| 1/4 teaspoon | 1 mL |
| 1/2 teaspoon | 2 mL |
| 1 teaspoon | 5 mL |
| 1 tablespoon = 3 teaspoons | 15 mL |
| 2 tablespoons = 1 fluid ounce | 30 mL |
| 1/4 cup | 60 mL |
| 1/3 cup | 75 mL |
| 1/2 cup = 4 fluid ounces | 125 mL |
| 1 cup = 8 fluid ounces | 250 mL |
| 2 cups = 1 pint =16 fluid ounces | 500 mL |
| 4 cups = 1 quart | 1 L |

### Weights

| | |
|---|---|
| 1 ounce | 30 g |
| 4 ounces | 120 g |
| 8 ounces | 225 g |
| 16 ounces = 1 pound | 450 g |

### Oven Temperatures

| | |
|---|---|
| 300° F | 150° C |
| 325° F | 160° C |
| 350° F | 180° C |
| 375° F | 190° C |
| 400° F | 200° C |
| 450° F | 230° C |

### Baking Pan Sizes

*Square*

| | |
|---|---|
| 8x8x2 inches | 2 L = 20x20x5 cm |
| 9x9x2 inches | 2.5 L = 23x23x5 cm |

*Rectangular*

| | |
|---|---|
| 13x9x2 inches | 3.5 L = 33x23x5 cm |

*Loaf*

| | |
|---|---|
| 9x5x3 inches | 2 L = 23x13x7 cm |

*Round*

| | |
|---|---|
| 8x1-1/2 inches | 1.2 L = 20x4 cm |
| 9x1-1/2 inches | 1.5 L = 23x4 cm |